Mark G. Boyer

Breathing Deeply of God's New Life:

Preparing Spiritually for
the Sacraments of Initiation

ST. ANTHONY
MESSENGER
PRESS

CINCINNATI, OHIO

*To Mary Ann Ackerson,
my "second mother"*

Nihil Obstat: Rev. Hilarion Kistner, O.F.M.
          Rev. Robert J. Buschmiller

Imprimi Potest: Rev. John Bok, O.F.M.
          Provincial

Imprimatur: +James H. Garland, V.G.
          Archdiocese of Cincinnati
          July 9, 1992

The *nihil obstat* and *imprimatur* are a declaration that a book is considered
to be free from doctrinal or moral error. It is not implied that those who
have granted the *nihil obstat* and *imprimatur* agree with the contents,
opinions or statements expressed.

Cover and book design by Julie Lonneman
Cover calligraphy by Patti Paulus

ISBN 0-86716-163-9

Published by St. Anthony Messenger Press
Printed in the U.S.A.

Contents

"In the sacraments of Christian initiation we are freed from the power of darkness and joined to Christ's death, burial, and resurrection. We receive the Spirit of filial adoption and are part of the entire people of God in the celebration of the memorial of the Lord's death and resurrection.

"Baptism incorporates us into Christ and forms us into God's people. This first sacrament pardons all our sins, rescues us from the power of darkness, and brings us to the dignity of adopted children, a new creation through water and the Holy Spirit. Hence we are called and are indeed the children of God.

"By signing us with the gift of the Spirit, confirmation makes us more completely the image of the Lord and fills us with the Holy Spirit, so that we may bear witness to him before all the world and work to bring the Body of Christ to its fullness as soon as possible.

"Finally, coming to the table of the eucharist, we eat the flesh and drink the blood of the Son of Man so that we may have eternal life and show forth the unity of God's people. By offering ourselves with Christ, we share in the universal sacrifice, that is, the entire community of the redeemed offered to God by their High Priest, and we pray for a greater outpouring of the Holy Spirit so that the whole human race may be brought into the unity of God's family.

"Thus the three sacraments of Christian initiation closely combine to bring us, the faithful of Christ, to his full stature and enable us to carry out the mission of the entire people of God in the Church and the world."

Christian Initiation, General Introduction, pars. 1-2

Introduction

The title of this book states its purpose. First, it is to be used by you to prepare to celebrate the various component rites, the ceremonial words and actions which mark the completion of one stage of your Christian growth and the beginning of a new level of development—of the Rite of Christian Initiation of Adults (RCIA).

Christian initiation is a gradual process of incorporating you into the Catholic Church. It begins with your curiosity and inquiry, moves on to a period of information and formation and then progresses to a shorter time of intense preparation for acceptance into the Church. After this goal is accomplished, a final period is devoted to further spiritual growth and community life.

This book is not a preparation for the initiation process nor is it designed for group meetings of those involved in the process. Rather, it is meant for you as you prepare spiritually for the Rite of Christian Initiation of Adults.

In a world where everything is instant from morning coffee to evening tea, it seems there is no reason to prepare. There is nothing instant, however, about your relationship to a community of believers and its corporate relationship with God. This relationship must be prepared for and developed.

You must prepare spiritually. The root of spirituality is spirit, a biblical reference to the breath of God. God breathes life into you. Spirituality is inhaling deeply of this breath and becoming aware of the rhythm of God's spirit in your lifetime pilgrimage of faith.

As you move through the stages of the initiation process, you join the community of believers in marking these steps with special rituals—rites or ceremonies consisting of words and actions. All of the rites of the RCIA are grounded in and centered on the word of God.

In addition, this work is a resource book. It contains a supply of scriptural selections, quotations from the English translation of the *Rite of Christian Initiation of Adults,* reflections, meditation questions, prayers and journaling exercises for you as you prepare to celebrate the various rites of the RCIA process.

The Initiation Process

The process of Christian initiation is designed primarily for those who have not been baptized. If you have already been baptized into another Christian community and now seek full communion with the Catholic Church, you participate in a slightly different process, which will unfold during the weeks ahead. By baptism you have already become a member of the Church and a child of God. Your conversion is based on the baptism you have already received. Now you will develop the effects of it and prepare for full union with the Catholic Church. Most likely you will join those who have not been baptized for parts of the process, especially group meetings and some of the rites.

The process for both the baptized and the non-baptized consists of information and formation. Information means religious education, commonly called catechesis or religious instruction. Through lecture, discussion and reading, you receive the necessary information about Roman Catholicism.

Formation focuses on being molded into a new way of life through ritual or ceremony. Like clay molded by the potter, you are formed according to the values of Jesus by those who guide you—sponsors.

Sponsors are those Roman Catholics who already know you and are willing to assist you at the beginning of the initiation process. They function as witnesses to your moral character, faith and intention. In other words, by your sponsor's example, you should be motivated to embrace the lifetime business of reshaping your life.

Then, from the informational or catechetical perspective, one stage of the initiation process is completed when you have studied and learned the instruction as it is given by your catechist. From the formational or ritual perspective, you complete one stage and begin another when you participate in a specific rite. The formational dimension of the initiation process lasts forever.

During all of this preparation, the spiritual dimension of the rites can easily be overlooked by everyone involved in the process. This spiritual aspect is the need this book addresses.

How to Use This Book

This work is intended to be used primarily during Lent, the forty days preceding Easter, and during the Easter Season, the fifty days following Easter Sunday and ending with Pentecost Sunday.

After you are accepted as a catechumen (one who wishes to become a Catholic and one who has been accepted by the Church to complete the information and formation processes), on the first Sunday of Lent you are elected—chosen to enter more intensely into preparation for full acceptance into the Church during the Easter Vigil. This book provides exercises for each of the rites associated with these steps.

During the Easter Season your catechist will teach you how to use this book and grow into a deeper understanding of the sacraments of initiation—Baptism, Confirmation and the Holy Eucharist.

As directed by your catechist, you may be asked to share the fruit of the harvest of your reflection with others at group meetings during the Lenten and Easter seasons.

Your catechist is responsible for guiding your use of this book. He or she will announce which sections are to be read and prepared and which parts are to be shared with others.

While this book is not meant to be catechetical, that is doctrinal, it does contain some teaching. Your catechist who instructs you in the basic teachings of the Roman Catholic Church will find some sections of this work useful in preparing you to celebrate the various rites of the RCIA. Also, your catechist may use some of the reflections, meditation questions and journaling exercises as discussion starters for group meetings.

Your sponsors may share portions of this book or work with you on certain sections, as directed by your catechist.

Godparents, those who show you how to practice the gospel in both your personal and social life during the last weeks of your preparation, can use the exercises in this work and discuss the results with you.

Presiders, usually deacons and priests who lead the various religious ceremonies associated with the process, will find a treasure chest of material for homilies or sermons, and instruction based on the word of God. They can adapt the reflections to meet their needs. Furthermore, a presider's meditations and journaling can be the stepping-stone to sharing his own ongoing pilgrimage of faith with you.

In general, any fully-initiated members of the Church will find resources in this book to help them prepare privately for the community celebration of the RCIA's rites. Especially during Lent, the faithful will want to use this book to prepare to renew their baptismal promises during the Easter Vigil. During the Easter Season they can use this book to reflect on the meaning of their call to live Catholic Christian lives.

Fully initiated Catholics may join with other Catholics in small groups during Lent and Easter and use this work to discuss and share the results of their prayer, reflection and journaling as they continue their lifetime pilgrimage of faith.

By using the six-part process, explained below, catechumens, the elect, candidates for full communion, catechists, sponsors, godparents, presiders and the fully initiated can reflect on the word of God and enrich each others' lives.

The Six-Part Process

The Scriptures employed in the celebration of each rite of the RCIA are the basis for this work. The six-part process stems from and is grounded in the word of God.

First, selections from Scripture for each rite of the RCIA are presented. Second, a quotation from the English translation of the *Rite of Christian Initation of Adults* has been selected to complement the Scripture choice or develop a deeper understanding of it. The instructive material in the *RCIA* is a source for reflection, meditation and guidance.

A reflection forms the third part of the process. Assuming that spirituality is the breath of God in you, the reflection presents ideas about how you might approach the Scripture passage and *RCIA* quotation. The reflection develops key themes, images and words found in the Scripture selection and the provided quotation.

The fourth part, the meditation, consists of a question or a series of questions. It usually asks you to think about a recent experience of your life and identify how God was present, breathing and acting in your life.

The meditation question is for thinking, although this doesn't exclude the possibility of you recording some of your meditative thoughts. The point of the meditation, which should last ten to fifteen minutes, is to see God's activity in the more recent, ordinary events of your life.

The fifth part of the process is a prayer. It summarizes the ideas, themes and images in the Scripture passage and the *RCIA* quotation developed in the reflection and upon which you meditated.

The prayers are personal. After praising God for a particular gift or call in the past, you, the pray-er, petition for a similar gift or call in the present, asking God to continue acting in your life.

Finally, a journal exercise is provided. This activity is meant to be written in a notebook or journal. The exercise asks you to review the major events and experiences of your life and pinpoint how God has been leading and guiding you. It asks you to journey backward and mine the rich veins of your experiences of God.

The journal questions flow out of, build on and are designed to expand the meditation. It is hoped they will awaken or raise your consciousness of God's activity in your life in the past, no matter if you were aware of it at that time or not. Your future pilgrimage is conditioned by your past. This exercise is meant to take twenty-five to thirty minutes.

When the specific rite is finally celebrated, you will be prepared spiritually for it. The celebration of the rite will be the culmination of all of your past experiences of God, while simultaneously looking toward the future and expecting God to continue to breathe deeply in your life through daily, ordinary experiences.

Criteria for Selection of Scripture

The *RCIA* uses the lectionary's (a book of short biblical readings) three-year cycle (simply identified as "A" for selections from Mark's Gospel, "B" from Matthew's Gospel and "C" from Luke's Gospel) of Scripture passages for Sunday Masses. In other words, you will hear the same Scripture passage once every three years.

Your catechist, presider and other liturgical planners will be working together to ensure that the Scriptures chosen for a particular rite of the RCIA are the same as those assigned to you as you prepare to celebrate the rite.

The Scriptures have been chosen according to the following criteria:

Two Scripture passages are assigned for the Rite of Acceptance into the Order of Catechumens, the ceremony in which candidates publicly declare their intention to join the Church. Both of these selections are treated in this book.

The Rite of Election or Enrollment of Names is the ceremony which begins the intense and final period of preparation for full initiation into the Church. This rite usually takes place on the First Sunday of Lent; hence, all three readings for all three cycles are developed in this book.

You should use only the exercises for the present cycle (e.g., Cycle A: 1993, 1996, 1999, etc.; Cycle B: 1994, 1997, 2000, etc.; Cycle C: 1995, 1998, 2001, etc.).

The First Scrutiny, a public prayer for your continuing conversion and repentance, is usually celebrated on the Third Sunday of Lent; the readings from Cycle A are recommended when this rite is celebrated. All three readings for the Third Sunday of Lent, Cycle A, are treated in this work.

Sometime during the Third Week of Lent, the Presentation of the Creed, the Church's summary of faith, is usually celebrated. Five readings are given from which a choice of one has been made and developed in this book.

The Second Scrutiny is usually celebrated on the Fourth Sunday of Lent and, like the First Scrutiny, the readings from Cycle A are recommended. All three readings for the Fourth Sunday of Lent, Cycle A, are treated in this book.

Usually, on the Fifth Sunday of Lent, the Third Scrutiny is celebrated using the readings from Cycle A. All three readings for the Fifth Sunday of Lent, Cycle A, are treated.

Sometime during the Fifth Week of Lent, the Presentation of the Lord's Prayer, the Church's most valued prayer, is usually celebrated. For this rite four readings are provided from which one has been chosen and developed.

On Holy Saturday morning or early afternoon, certain Preparation Rites for the Easter Vigil can be celebrated. Two Scripture passages are provided; one has been chosen and developed for the Recitation of the Creed, the public proclamation of your faith in preparation for your full initiation into the Church during the Easter Vigil. One reading is provided for the Ephphetha Rite, a ritual expressing your need for God's grace in order to hear God's word and profess it; it is treated in this book.

In order to prepare for the celebration of the sacraments of initiation—Baptism, Confirmation, the Holy Eucharist— during the Easter Vigil, all eight readings which precede the Gospel have been treated. Some of these will be assigned by your catechist, dependent upon which Scriptures are selected for public proclamation during the Easter Vigil.

Since the current cycle dictates which Gospel is proclaimed during the Easter Vigil, the Gospel for each of the three cycles is provided and developed. Only the process for the Gospel of the current cycle should be used.

As your catechist directs, Scripture passages not used during the Easter Vigil can be used at other times during the initiation process, especially during the Period of Postbaptismal Catechesis or Mystagogy, the fifty-day period of your ongoing formation after Easter. During this period, which corresponds to the Easter Season, twenty-seven Scripture passages have been chosen: nine selections are provided for reflection on the Sacrament of Baptism, nine for reflection on Confirmation and nine for reflection on the Holy Eucharist.

These sections are designed to help you continue to develop your faith and understanding of the sacraments of initiation. While they are intended to be used during the Easter Season, your catechist may choose a selection to be used at another time or during a group session devoted to Baptism, Confirmation or Eucharist.

This book concludes with a selection for use on Pentecost Sunday, which brings the Easter Season to a close. This final exercise should be used at the last gathering of all persons involved in the official process.

It is important to note that this book is not designed to be the content of the information dimension of the initiation process. It is to be used for preparation to celebrate the rites of the RCIA, which contain a public proclamation of God's word. Through your reflection, meditation and journaling activities, you will be prepared spiritually to celebrate each rite.

Celebrations of the Word of God

Throughout the periods of information and formation, the *RCIA* recommends that celebrations of the word of God be held.

"During the period of the catechumenate there should be celebrations of the word of God that accord with the liturgical season and that contribute to the instruction of the catechumens and the needs of the community. These celebrations of the word are: first, celebrations held specially for the catechumens; second, participation in the liturgy of the word at the Sunday Mass; third, celebrations held in connection with catechetical instruction." (par. 81)

A model is provided for these celebrations in the *RCIA*.[1]

Your catechist can use material from this book for the opening prayer of group sessions, as well as for continued reflection and sharing during the periods of the catechumenate and Lent, when after the homily during Mass, you are dismissed to continue to ponder the meaning of the word of God and identify the activity of God in your life.

During the Easter Season, your catechist may assign selections to be used in a celebration of the word of God during a group meeting. Or, daily you may pick individual parts to use for your private prayer.

In general, your catechist should make a selection from this book and assign it to you to be used in your preparation for your next gathering. At that time, a public proclamation of the word of God can be given with large- or small-group sharing taking place among the members of your group.

A presider might preach a homily on the text chosen by the catechist, share a personal reflection and invite a response from you.

Since the book is a resource, there is no limit to the ways in which it can be used as a spiritual tool in preparing to celebrate the rites of the RCIA and in celebrations of the word of God, an integral part of the initiation process.

It is my hope that you who prepare for the sacraments of initiation and full union with the Catholic Church, as well as all of those who assist you, will grow in the spirituality of

---

[1] *Rite of Christian Initiation of Adults,* International Committee on English in the Liturgy, 1985, pars. 85-89.

the pilgrim people of God and breathe deeply of God's new and abundant life as you are formed into the likeness of the risen Christ by the Holy Spirit.

Chapter One

Rite of Acceptance Into the Order of Catechumens

"The first period consists of inquiry on the part of the
candidates and of evangelization and the
precatechumenate on the part of the Church. It ends with
the rite of acceptance into the order of catechumens"
(*RCIA*, par. 7:1).

"The second period, which begins with the rite of
acceptance into the order of catechumens and may last for
several years, includes catechesis and the rites connected
with catechesis. It comes to an end on the day of election"
(*RCIA*, par. 7:2).

"The first step: reaching the point of initial conversion and
wishing to become Christian, [candidates] are accepted as
catechumens by the Church" (*RCIA*, par. 6:1).

Leaving Home

Scripture "The LORD said to Abram: 'Go forth from the land of your kinsfolk and from your father's house to a land that I will show you....' Abram went as the LORD directed him..." (Genesis 12:1, 4).

RCIA "The prerequisite for making this first step is that the beginnings of the spiritual life and the fundamentals of Christian teaching have taken root in the candidates. Thus there must be evidence of the first faith that was conceived during the period of evangelization and precatechumenate and of an initial conversion and intention to change their lives and to enter into a relationship with God in Christ" (par. 42).

Reflection Leaving home is a traumatic experience for most people. Such leave-taking may be a child going to a day-care center every morning, an adolescent going away to a boarding school, a young adult going away to college or a whole family moving from one city to another.

There is nothing sure about leaving home, that other womb, that place of security. However, sooner or later you have to leave home and venture forth into the world where new people, new experiences and new ways of life await you. While leave-taking never becomes easy, it does become more manageable as you engage in it repeatedly throughout your life.

Becoming a catechumen involves some leave-taking. In one way, you leave one way of life and choose to walk still more lovingly on the path that is the way of Jesus. You enter into the new home of an ongoing life of conversion in the image of Jesus.

God calls you to leave home, just as he called Abram to leave his people and inheritance. Abram obeyed; he did not know what awaited him, but he trusted in the God who promised him a new and fuller life. Likewise, you do not know what a new spiritual life will bring your way, but you trust in the promise of God.

Meditation When did you most recently have a "leaving home" experience? What were your fears? What new life did you discover in your new home?

Prayer God of Abram, once you spoke to your servant and called him to leave the home of his father and to journey to a new land. You promised to make of him a great nation and to make his name a blessing. Believing in your word, Abram obeyed you. Give me the courage to leave behind the security of my old home that I might answer your call to journey to a new spiritual life of conversion. Draw me closer into the inner circle of your love.

Journal Make a list of what you consider to be the three most traumatic leave-taking experiences of your life. Whom or what did you leave? What changes took place in your life as a result of leaving home?

Curiosity

Scripture "...John [the Baptist] was...with two of his disciples, and as he watched Jesus walk by, he said, 'Behold, the Lamb of God.' The two disciples heard what he said and followed Jesus. Jesus turned and saw them following him and said to them, 'What are you looking for?' They said to him, 'Rabbi' (which translated means Teacher), 'where are you staying?' He said to them, 'Come, and you will see.' So they went and saw where he was staying, and they stayed with him that day" (John 1:35-39).

RCIA "The rite that is called the rite of acceptance into the order of catechumens is of the utmost importance. Assembling publicly for the first time, the candidates who have completed the period of the precatechumenate declare their intention to the Church and the Church in turn, carrying out its apostolic mission, accepts them as persons who intend to become its members" (par. 41).

Reflection You are curious. You satisfy your curiosity by dropping hints or posing questions. Curiosity is satisfied by roaming through a department store and seeing and touching the latest styles in clothing. You may watch television talk shows or read books to satisfy your curiosity about various topics.

Maybe the man who aroused the most curiosity ever was Jesus of Nazareth. People with whom he lived in the first century found him extremely intriguing. After he was put to death and raised from the dead many more people began to give in to their curiosity and investigate his life and teachings.

A catechumen is a person who is curious about Jesus. The Church, the new and public Body of Christ, invites you, the curious, to come and see, just as Jesus in John's Gospel invites the two disciples to join him. You enter into a lifetime pilgrimage of delving deeper and deeper into the meaning of Jesus, while the Church pledges to support your journey as the rest of her members continue their curious search.

You and the Church publicly promise to continue the quest for the Teacher and the never-ending process of changing your life according to his teaching.

Meditation Why do you want to become a catechumen and enter the Catholic Church? What are you curiously seeking?

Prayer God of the curious, you sent John the Baptist to prepare the way for the coming of your Son, Jesus, the Lamb of God. John pointed him out to his own disciples, who, in turn, curiously followed him. Through my curiosity, deepen my hunger to learn the teachings of Jesus. Through the curiosity of the other members of the Church, support me in converting my life.

Journal Make a list of three experiences of your life when you were extremely curious. What did you learn from each experience? How did each experience change your life?

Chapter Two

Rite of Election or Enrollment of Names

"The third and much shorter period, which follows the rite of
election, ordinarily coincides with the Lenten preparation
for the Easter celebration and the sacraments of initiation.
It is a time of purification and enlightenment and includes
the celebration of the rites belonging to this period" (*RCIA*,
par. 7:3).

"The second step: having progressed in faith and nearly
completed the catechumenate, [catechumens] are
accepted into a more intense preparation for the
sacraments of initiation" (*RCIA*, par. 6:2).

The First Sunday of Lent
Cycle A (1993, 1996, 1999, etc.)

Decisions

Scripture "The serpent asked the woman, 'Did God really tell you not to eat from any of the trees in the garden?' The woman answered the serpent: 'We may eat of the fruit of the trees in the garden; it is only about the fruit of the tree in the middle of the garden that God said, "You shall not eat it or even touch it, lest you die."' But the serpent said to the woman: 'You certainly will not die! No, God knows well that the moment you eat of it your eyes will be opened and you will be like gods who know what is good and what is bad' " (Genesis 3:1-5).

RCIA "Since this transition [from the old to a new nature made perfect in Christ] brings with it a progressive change of outlook and conduct, it should become manifest by means of its social consequences and it should develop gradually during the period of the catechumenate. Since the Lord in whom [the catechumens] believe is a sign of contradiction, the newly converted often experience divisions and separations, but they also taste the joy that God gives without measure" (par. 75:2).

Reflection Every day you have to make decisions. The first decision comes with answering the buzz of the alarm clock; you can either turn it off, roll over and go back to sleep, or decide to get up, shower, dress and begin a new day.

Parents must make decisions concerning their children. Who will pick up Mary after school? Who will attend John's baseball or basketball game? Whose turn is it to help with homework assignments or to make dinner?

Some decisions are small and made without a lot of

thought. Other decisions, like brick walls, stop you for a period of time. Should I accept that job offer, even though it means moving to a new city? Should we build or buy a new house? Can we afford a new car?

Your decision to join the Church is one of your most important. It should not be made lightly or quickly. Such a decision involves a willingness to change your outlook—the way you perceive the world and your conduct—your life-style. When you join the Church, you are deciding to embrace Jesus' outlook and act as Jesus did.

A decision to join the Church is one which involves putting to death the serpent that lurks in each of us, that part of ourselves that desires to *be* a god instead of being obedient to God. Jesus' way is a contradiction in a world in which every one of us seeks control. Jesus relinquished all power and was obedient to God all the way to the cross. By following the way of Jesus you will experience division and separation. Your decision should not be made lightly.

Meditation What is your primary reason for wanting to join the Church?

Prayer Lord God, you once formed man and woman out of the clay of the ground and blew into their nostrils the breath of life. Then you bestowed upon them your greatest gifts. However, they decided to seek their own power instead of being obedient to your will. As I seek to follow in the obedient footsteps of Jesus, change my outlook and conduct.

Journal Identify three divisions or separations that might occur in your life as a result of your decision to join the Church. How do you plan to cope with each one?

From Death to Grace

Scripture "...[J]ust as through one transgression condemnation came upon all, so through one righteous act acquittal and life came to all. For just as through the disobedience of one person the many were made sinners, so through the obedience of one the many will be made righteous" (Romans 5:18-19).

RCIA "...[T]he newly converted set out on a spiritual journey. Already sharing through faith in the mystery of Christ's death and resurrection, they pass from the old to a new nature made perfect in Christ" (par. 75:2).

Reflection The Book of Genesis has two creation stories. The first narrates the world being created in six days and God resting on the seventh day. The second relates the disobedience of the first man and woman. This transgression of God's commandment was the opened door through which sin and death entered the world. The consequence of sin is death, according to the account.

But God was not satisfied with the entrance of sin and death into the world, so God offered the gift of reconciliation through the obedience of Jesus, the Son. God did the necessary reconciling with us through Jesus. This gift is called grace; it acquits all of us.

God offers the gift of grace to each of us. Yet, God does not take away our freedom to reject this precious gift. God has made all of us acceptable—this is called justification—through the obedient suffering, death and resurrection of Jesus.

If you accept this gift of God, you are baptized into the suffering, death and resurrection of Jesus. Thus, you continue a spiritual journey of learning how to continually be obedient to God, like Jesus, and reject sinful disobedience. This doesn't happen in an instant, but it is a gradual transformation through a lifetime of conversion.

Meditation What three steps have you taken in your spiritual journey in obedience to God?

Prayer Righteous God, you reconciled sinful humanity to yourself through the obedient suffering, death and resurrection of Jesus. Through the waters of baptism you called me to die with him so that I can share in his new life. Continue the obedient process of transformation in me. Bring me to perfection in the Lord Jesus Christ, your Son.

Journal Outline the major steps of your spiritual journey. What are your major obedient experiences? What are your major disobedient experiences?

Conversion

Scripture "...Jesus was led by the Spirit into the desert to be tempted by the devil. He fasted for forty days and forty nights, and afterwards he was hungry. The tempter approached and said to him, 'If you are the Son of God, command that these stones become loaves of bread.' He said in reply, 'It is written:

> 'One does not live by bread alone, but by every word that comes forth from the mouth of God' "
> (Matthew 4:1-4).

RCIA "Before the rite of election is celebrated, the catechumens are expected to have undergone a conversion in mind and in action and to have developed a sufficient acquaintance with Christian teaching as well as a spirit of faith and charity" (par. 120).

Reflection The word "conversion" means change or alteration. Daily, you can witness cosmetic conversions as people you know change the style of their hair, you observe a new street being built through a vacant field or you paint your house a different color. These types of external alterations surround us.

The type of conversion demanded of you here is quite different. First, it involves a conversion of mind, probably the most difficult type of change. Conversion of mind involves values, perspective and attitude. You who want to become a Catholic must begin to think in a different way by adopting the values of the right to life, community and sacraments. These values create a perspective, a new way to view the world. They also affect your attitude and how you approach the various issues that present themselves in the course of a day.

Second, you are asked to make a conversion of action. Once authentic Christian values are embraced, your actions demonstrate these values. For example, you uphold the right of every person to life and you do not support any social system that tries to remove this value.

You are found to be involved in the community of believers, especially in work with those on society's fringes. This may take the form of time volunteered in the local soup kitchen, work on the social concerns committee of your parish or helping to administer a food pantry.

The value of the Church's sacraments is acted out in your life through your preparation for celebration. Your presence is recognized when the local Church community gathers together. Even though you may share only minimally, you are found to be present to hear the word of God, which excites a desire to share completely as you look forward to the day of your complete initiation into the Church.

Throughout your life, you will be confronted with the temptation, like Jesus, to turn back, to use your power in the old ways, to return to life as it once was. But conversion of mind and action sets you on a new pilgrimage, during which you must have faith in the word of God.

Meditation What are the most important conversions of mind and action that have taken place in your life?

Prayer God of conversion, your Spirit led your Son into the desert to be tempted by the devil so that you might strengthen him for his mission to your people. Send me an abundance of your grace that I might be converted in heart and action. Help me to embrace the values of your kingdom.

Journal Make a list of what you consider authentic Christian values. For each value identify what action you need to take to show you have fully embraced the value.

First Sunday of Lent
Cycle B (1994, 1997, 2000, etc.)

Covenant

Scripture "God said to Noah and to his sons with him: 'See, I am now establishing my covenant with you and your descendants after you and with every living creature that was with you: all the birds, and the various tame and wild animals that were with you and came out of the ark.... This is the sign that I am giving for all ages to come, of the covenant between me and you and every living creature with you: I set my bow in the clouds to serve as a sign of the covenant between me and the earth' " (Genesis 9:8-10, 12-13).

RCIA "This step is called election because the acceptance made by the Church is founded on the election by God, in whose name the Church acts. The step is also called the enrollment of names because as a pledge of fidelity the candidates inscribe their names in the book that lists those who have been chosen for initiation" (par. 119).

Reflection A contract differs from a covenant. A contract is a legal document that binds two parties in a specific arrangement for a specified time. For example, one person agrees to buy five acres of land from another person. The contract stipulates who is involved in the transaction, what monies are being exchanged for what piece of property and for what period of time ownership will be transferred.

However, in a covenant, God, a certainly greater party when compared to any human being, decides to enter into a specific agreement with us, who have nothing to offer in return except a willingness to obey the terms of God's offer. It is important to note that God makes the first move in a covenant.

The first covenant the Bible mentions is the one God entered into with Noah, his family and every living creature. It consisted of a promise by God to never again deluge the earth with water. As a sign of the covenant, any time a rainbow appeared in the sky both parties promised to remember the everlasting pact. Thus, both God and people would remain faithful to each other.

Later, the Bible relates covenant-making ceremonies with Abraham, Moses and the new covenant sealed in Jesus' blood. In each of these, God makes the first move and offers to people what they cannot obtain on their own.

The Church, the assembly of believers, acts in the name of God when catechumens, such as yourself, are elected. The Church extends the new covenant to you who are willing to accept it. The Church believes that God has already chosen you—that is, God has already made the first move—and accepts your pledge of fidelity to the covenant. Bound together by God, those who have already accepted the new covenant and you who are preparing to be fully initiated into it promise to help each other to remain faithful.

Meditation What has God offered you in covenant that you were unable to achieve on your own?

Prayer God of the covenant, after the earth was deluged with the great flood, you set your bow in the sky as a sign to Noah that never again would water destroy creation. With Abraham you entered into a covenant to make his name great and his descendants as numerous as the sands on the seashore. With Moses, you bound yourself to the chosen people in a covenant-making ceremony of blood. In the blood of Jesus, you established the new covenant in which you invited all people to share. Keep me faithful to my calling and bring me to the eternal life of Jesus.

Journal What do you consider to be the terms of the covenant among you, the community of believers and God?

Water

Scripture "...God patiently waited in the days of Noah during the building of the ark, in which a few persons, eight in all, were saved through water. This prefigured baptism, which saves you now. It is not a removal of dirt from the body but an appeal to God for a clear conscience, through the resurrection of Jesus Christ, who has gone into heaven and is at the right hand of God,..." (1 Peter 3:20-22).

RCIA "The Church, like a mother, helps the catechumens on their journey by means of suitable liturgical rites, which purify the catechumens little by little and strengthen them with God's blessing.... [T]hey must await their baptism, which will join them to God's priestly people and empower them to participate in Christ's new worship" (par. 75:3).

Reflection Water is so common it is taken for granted—until there is a flood or a drought. A flood is a destructive force; it washes away roads, homes and people. It eliminates bridges and changes the course of rivers and streams. It can destroy spring crops in the fields. Every person and animal on the earth was destroyed by the great flood, except Noah, his family and the animals he took in the ark.

Although it is destructive, water is also life-giving. During a drought, we see more than ever the need for water for green lawns and abundant harvests. Without water, we dehydrate and die. For nine months in your mother's womb, you were surrounded by life-giving and life-protecting water. The people and animals in Noah's ark were saved through the water of the great flood.

This dual characteristic of water—at once destructive and saving—is celebrated in the Sacrament of Baptism. Your old life is submerged as you rise from the death-dealing waters to be born again.

Also, baptism is at one and the same time the culmination of the catechumenal journey and the beginning of the pilgrimage with the whole Christian community. You prepare for baptism with the help of the members of the Church, who have already experienced its destructive and saving power. Like a parent, the members of the Church walk with you as you seek to enter into the death and resurrection of Jesus. They help you learn how to die in the baptismal tomb and rise to new life.

Baptism fully immerses you into the Christian community. You, then, will become responsible for helping others learn the mystery of the destructive and life-giving characteristics of water.

Meditation What was your most recent experience of water as a destructive force? What was your most recent experience of water as a life-giving force?

Prayer God of the waters, once your Spirit hovered over the primeval chaotic water and brought forth the life of creation. When the power of sin overwhelmed the world, you washed it clean with the waters of the great flood, while Noah and those with him in the ark were saved. Guide me in my journey of preparation for this great sacrament of salvation. Wash away all sin from my life and bring me to new birth through the resurrection of Jesus Christ.

Journal What three habits, behaviors or ways of responding need to be destroyed in your life as you prepare for baptism? What new habits, behaviors or ways of responding can you replace these with?

Good News

Scripture "After John had been arrested, Jesus came to Galilee proclaiming the gospel of God: 'This is the time of fulfillment. The kingdom of God is at hand. Repent, and believe in the gospel' " (Mark 1:14-15).

RCIA "The time spent in the catechumenate should be long enough—several years if necessary—for the conversion and faith of the catechumens to become strong. By their formation in the entire Christian life and a sufficiently prolonged probation the catechumens are properly initiated into the mysteries of salvation and the practice of an evangelical way of life" (par. 76).

Reflection The word "gospel" usually means "good news." However, the Greek word from which the English "gospel" is translated was used in ancient times as "good news of a victory" to indicate that one's forces had defeated one's enemies.

The author of Mark's Gospel is the only author who calls his work a "gospel." The author of Matthew's Gospel calls his work a "book"; the author of Luke's Gospel calls his work a "narrative"; and the author of John's Gospel never gives his work a title.

Thus, for the author of Mark's Gospel, what is the "good news of the victory"? The "good news of the victory" is that God has kept his promise to send the Messiah, the Anointed One. Once the kingship was eliminated, the people of Israel began to place their hope in the promise that God would raise up a warrior-king from the line of David. He would restore the political power and the boundaries of Israel as they had been during David's glorious reign.

However, Jesus' picture did not match this Davidic portrait. He did not participate in political power struggles nor did he restore Israel's borders. Yet, according to Mark's Gospel, he was the fulfillment of God's promises. He was the embodiment of God's kingdom; in the person of Jesus, God was reigning over his people. This new type of kingdom is one in which God is found in the suffering and death (abandonment) of his own Son!

Repentance is necessary to participate in this kingdom. The call to repent calls you to turn from the old ways of perceiving reality and embrace the new. In Mark's Gospel this means finding God in abandonment.

The response to Mark's "good news of the victory" also involves belief in it. You must believe God is found where most people think God should not be—on the cross. If you look for political power, the defeat of the cross holds little appeal. It is hard to believe, if not impossible, that the God of Israel has established his kingdom and won the victory on a cross!

No wonder, then, it may take you several years to be converted and for your faith to become strong. Initiation into the Church is a step-by-step process that cannot be rushed. It demands a radical turning away from the old presupposition that God is a God of power and might to the new premise that God is a God of powerful powerlessness. Once this mystery is embraced, you can begin to discover God in your moments of abandonment.

Meditation In which recent experience of abandonment (powerlessness) did you experience the kingdom of God in your life? Explain.

Prayer God of the kingdom, you sent Jesus, your Son, to announce the good news that your reign had begun in the powerlessness of the world. His call to repent and believe in the gospel continues to echo this day. Enlighten my mind as I strive to understand and embrace this mystery. Strengthen my faith in the good news of the victory that you are present in my moments of helplessness and abandonment.

Journal Make a list of the three major occasions in your life when you felt totally abandoned by God or others. As you look back on these experiences, identify how God was present and active in your powerlessness. In other words, how did you experience the kingdom?

First Sunday of Lent
Cycle C (1995, 1998, 2001, etc.)

Memories

Scripture "...'My father was a wandering Aramean who went down to Egypt with a small household and lived there as an alien. But there he became a nation great, strong and numerous. When the Egyptians maltreated and oppressed us, imposing hard labor upon us, we cried to the LORD, the God of our fathers, and he heard our cry and saw our affliction, our toil and our oppression. He brought us out of Egypt with his strong hand and outstretched arm, with terrifying power, with signs and wonders; and bringing us into this country, he gave us this land flowing with milk and honey;...' " (Deuteronomy 26:5-9).

RCIA "The special celebrations of the word of God arranged for the benefit of the catechumens have as their main purpose:

1. to implant in their hearts the teachings they are receiving...,
2. to give them instruction and experience in the different aspects and ways of prayer;

27

3. to explain to them the signs, celebrations, and seasons of the liturgy;

4. to prepare them gradually to enter the worship assembly of the entire community" (par. 82).

Reflection You possess memories, recollections of past events, experiences, thoughts, encounters and so on. While you probably don't analyze your memories much, the most significant memories in your formation are remembered, and the least significant are usually forgotten.

For example, your memory of your first bicycle may be etched rather clearly on your mind. Like a videotape, you can review the scenes of going to the store, picking out the bicycle, bringing it home and riding it for the first time. This memory is important because it was an experience of freedom, like none ever experienced before. Undoubtedly, there have been many more experiences of freedom in your life, but this one stands out significantly and is remembered.

As you journey to complete initiation in the Church, you must be exposed to the collective memories of the community. These memories are those that form the Church in the ways of God. Both the events of the Old Testament and those of the New Testament are part of this collection of memories.

For example, the Book of Deuteronomy gives the formula that the offerer must use when making a thanksgiving offering to God after the harvest. Notice that the formula is a collection of memories. The offerer recites these with the offering to remember what God has done.

The ritual words call to mind Jacob's move to Egypt, the growth of his descendants, their enslavement by the Egyptians, their rescue by God and their inheritance of the promised land. Combined together, these events represent God's great deeds and the reason why people should make an offering from the harvest to God.

Meditation What do you think is the most important event from the life of Jesus that Christians need to remember?

Prayer God of memories, you never forget your people. You led your chosen servant, Jacob, to Egypt, where his descendants became a great nation. When they were afflicted with oppression, you rescued them and led them to the land you had promised their ancestors. Keep these memories alive in my heart. Continue to work your signs and wonders in my midst today. Never let me forget the saving death and resurrection of Jesus, your Son.

Journal Make a list of ten memories you think a follower of Jesus should never forget. Why do you think each is so important to remember?

Faith

Scripture "...If you confess with your mouth that Jesus is Lord and believe in your heart that God raised him from the dead, you will be saved. For one believes with the heart and so is justified, and one confesses with the mouth and so is saved" (Romans 10:9-10).

RCIA "From the day of their election and admission, the catechumens are called 'the elect.' They are also described as *competentes* ('co-petitioners'), because they are joined together in asking for and aspiring to receive the three sacraments of Christ and the gift of the Holy Spirit. They are also called *illuminandi* ('those who will be enlightened'), because baptism itself has been called *illuminatio* ('enlightenment') and it fills the newly baptized with the light of faith" (par. 124).

Reflection In the first century it was rather hazardous to declare that "Jesus is Lord." The Jew who made such a statement would be immediately accused of blasphemy; everyone knew that "God is the Lord." The Gentile who made such a statement would be accused of being a traitor to the state; every loyal citizen knew that

"Caesar is Lord."

Such a proclamation of faith, according to Paul's Letter to the Romans, is your demonstration that you have accepted God's offer of justifying grace brought about through the death and resurrection of Jesus. God has already saved you through Jesus' redemptive acts. It is up to you to accept God's offer of righteousness. Once accepted, you proclaim that "Jesus is Lord."

Just as God has chosen everyone to accept the free offer of grace and to respond with faith, so the Church chooses you, "the elect," from among the catechumens to begin an intense period of preparation for the sacraments of initiation. This election means you are not scared to confess with your mouth that Jesus is Lord at home, in the workplace and at play. It also means your faith is not something of social convenience or like clothes only worn on the outside; it means your faith has taken root in your heart, and motivates and inspires your every action.

The Church elects you individually and all catechumens collectively. While you continue your journey, the already-initiated lead you down the path of enlightenment in the ways of Jesus.

Meditation In which recent circumstance did you find yourself confessing that "Jesus is Lord" by what you said or did? Explain.

Prayer Righteous God, when people were lost in sin and could not find their way to you, you justified them through the blood of Jesus, your Son. Through his death and resurrection you offered all people the gift of righteous grace. Strengthen the faith which my lips profess, and make firm that which my heart believes. With others I confess that "Jesus is Lord."

Journal List three ways you can demonstrate your faith at home, work and play.

Evil

S c r i p t u r e "Filled with the holy Spirit, Jesus returned from the Jordan and was led by the Spirit into the desert for forty days, to be tempted by the devil.... [H]e took him up and showed him all the kingdoms of the world in a single instant. The devil said to him, 'I shall give to you all this power and their glory; for it has been handed over to me, and I may give it to whomever I wish. All this will be yours, if you worship me.' Jesus said to him in reply, 'It is written:

> You shall worship the Lord, your God, and him
> alone shall you serve' " (Luke 4:1-2, 5-8).

R C I A "The first or minor exorcisms have been composed in the form of petitions directly addressed to God. They draw the attention of the catechumens to the real nature of Christian life, the struggle between flesh and spirit, the importance of self-denial for reaching the blessedness of God's kingdom, and the unending need for God's help" (par. 90).

R e f l e c t i o n The series of movies which are known by their generic name "The Exorcist" have served to cloud the Church's stance toward exorcism. Certainly, the Church does not think you are possessed by the devil and your life is dominated by evil. However, the Church does believe evil exists and it needs to be confronted.

Evil is discovered as you struggle with flesh and spirit. The flesh can be tempted to concede to its desire for "more"—more food, more clothes, more gadgets in your home. The greed of the New World must confront the spirit of poverty of the Third World. When it does, a struggle will ensue.

Likewise, the flesh has no concern for the environment and sees it as only another commodity to be used. The spirit calls forth a deep respect for the earth and for the dignity of every human person who lives on our planet.

As you struggle with flesh and spirit you will see the homeless walking the streets in your town. The flesh asks, "Why don't they get a job like the rest of us?" The spirit confronts such apathy and asks, "What am I doing to help make this town a better place in which all people can live and have an equal opportunity to improve themselves?"

The flesh can also be tempted to concede to its desire for a premarital sexual union, cheat on a spouse in an extramarital affair or satisfy its lust through pornographic materials. In its struggle, the spirit calls you to respect the dignity of the body of every human being and the marital covenant and scorn anything that derides the beauty of human sexuality.

Evil can be found in the workplace, where you seek power and you are willing to do whatever is necessary to get it. Subtly you drop hints concerning the lack of organizational abilities or the lack of training of your fellow employees in order to get a promotion. Believing that you are worth more than you are being paid, you take home a few office supplies to compensate. Because of their love for power, many people "work" their way up the corporate ladder by effectively eliminating anyone who gets in their way.

Even Jesus had to face the power of evil. Absolute power, in exchange for worshiping evil, was offered to Jesus by the devil. It is easy to fall down and worship evil because it promises to give what we so ardently seek to have. Jesus, however, realized that the power that evil promised was empty and self defeating.

Prejudice is another evil that frequently manifests itself today. More often than not, it is done secretly. A family is denied a loan for a home in a particular neighborhood because of the color of their skin or ethnic background. A job-seeker is not given the position for which he or she is qualified because he or she is not white. Because of where they live, some people are not permitted in certain stores to shop. This is evil under the name of prejudice.

Self-denial is the practice of members of the Church. Self-denial counters evil. It is a discipline which reminds you that all power over others is illusory, only God possesses absolute power. Thus, only God is to be worshiped.

The prayers of exorcism for you are designed to open your eyes to see the spirit of evil. They ask God to guard you from error and sin. Only with God's help, which is more powerful than evil, can you attain the blessings of God's kingdom.

Meditation Most recently, where have you encountered evil? How did you deal with it?

Prayer God of all power, you always guard your people from the power of evil. You teach them to rely upon the guidance of the Spirit as they practice the discipline of self denial. Be with me when I struggle to do what is right and just. Fill me with your grace that I might be strengthened to walk in the footsteps of Jesus.

Journal Go through today's newspaper (or the most recent one you have) and make a list of every news article that exposes some evil. Name the evil and identify a way the evil could be eradicated.

Chapter Three

Rites Belonging to the Period of Purification and Enlightenment

"The period of purification and enlightenment, which the rite of election begins, customarily coincides with Lent. In the liturgy and liturgical catechesis of Lent the reminder of baptism already received or the preparation for its reception, as well as the theme of repentance, renews the entire community along with those being prepared to celebrate the paschal mystery, in which each of the elect will share through the sacraments of initiation. For both the elect and the local community, therefore, the Lenten season is a time for spiritual recollection in preparation for the celebration of the paschal mystery" (*RCIA*, par. 138).

"This is a period of more intense spiritual preparation, consisting more in interior reflection than in catechetical instruction, and is intended to purify minds and hearts of the elect as they search their own consciences and do penance. This period is intended as well to enlighten the minds and hearts of the elect with a deeper knowledge of Christ the Savior. The celebration of certain rites, particularly the scrutinies and the presentations, brings about this process of purification and enlightenment and extends it over the course of the entire Lenten season" (*RCIA*, par. 139).

First Scrutiny

(Third Sunday of Lent: Cycle A)

Strike the Rock

Scripture "...[I]n their thirst for water, the people grumbled against Moses.... So Moses cried out to the LORD.... The LORD answered Moses, 'Go over there in front of the people, along with some of the elders of Israel, holding in your hand, as you go, the staff with which you struck the river. I will be standing there in front of you on the rock in Horeb. Strike the rock, and the water will flow from it for the people to drink' " (Exodus 17:3-6).

RCIA "The blessings of the catechumens are a sign of God's love and of the Church's tender care. They are bestowed on the catechumens so that, even though they do not as yet have the grace of the sacraments, they may still receive from the Church courage, joy, and peace as they proceed along the difficult journey they have begun" (par. 95).

"The celebrant, with hands outstretched over the catechumens, says one of the...prayers. After the prayer of blessing, if this can be done conveniently, the catechumens come before the celebrant, who lays hands on them individually" (par. 97).

Reflection When you hear the word "rock," you think of an inanimate object. Rocks are the building blocks of mountains. Construction crews cut through rocks in order to build straight highways. Even in your backyard garden, you pick up a few rocks and toss them to the side during spring tilling.

People can be like rocks. We come in all shapes and sizes. Some personality types are harder than others. Some are more resistant to change than others. Getting bogged down in one place or with one set of ideas, we refuse to move or grow into new perspectives. We may even grumble about being stuck, but we see no way to get pried out of our rocky fastness.

Moses had to deal with grumbling rocks, the Israelites. They had made a successful escape from Egyptian slavery and were discovering the thirst of the desert. Instead of remembering the great act of God, they began to quarrel with Moses about being thirsty. Just as God had drawn the water of desire for freedom from the Israelites in the past, so now God decides to draw forth from them a stream of trust.

In their stubbornness and thirst, the people are like rocks. They cannot move. Their tongues are dry. They are tired and willing to give up the pursuit and just die where they are. What they need is a little refreshing courage and another injection of determination to continue their journey.

And this is what they get. God strikes the rock and water begins to flow. What is important to note is that God opens people to the river of grace. It doesn't flow into them, it flows out of them. They have to be made aware of the invisible loving hand of God stretched out over them in the visible person of Moses. Once this is accomplished, they realize again that God is in their midst, and, as they drink the rock's water, they drink of God's grace.

You are like a rock. The initial joy of beginning your journey of faith can quickly fade as you enter into the more difficult stages of conversion of life. You need to be reassured by the community of believers that water will continue to flow from within you. The blessings, given with the laying on of hands, remind you of God's love and the care of the whole Church for you.

The prayer of blessing is like Moses' staff, used to strike the rock of life's hardness. As it touches your heart, the courage, joy and peace of the pilgrimage of faith return. With the renewed strength from the flow of grace, you, the catechumen continue toward the sacraments of initiation.

Meditation When have you most recently experienced being like a rock? Whom did God use to touch you and cause you to flow with renewed strength?

Prayer God, our rock, when your people quarreled with Moses because there was no water for them to drink, you brought forth water from the rock. You stretched out your hand and strengthened them to continue their journey to the promised land. When I become as hard as rock, strike me with your presence. Awaken in me the flow of your grace. Lead me through my difficult journey of faith to the promised land of your kingdom.

Journal Make a list of all the ways you think you are like a rock. In which of these ways has God struck you and caused the water of grace to flow from you?

Willing to Die

Scripture "Indeed, only with difficulty does one die for a just person, though perhaps for a good person one might even find courage to die. But God proves his love for us in that while we were still sinners Christ died for us" (Romans 5:7-8).

RCIA "During the period of the catechumenate, a rite of anointing the catechumens, through use of the oil of catechumens, may be celebrated wherever this seems beneficial or desirable" (par. 98).

"Care is to be taken that the catechumens understand the

significance of the anointing with oil. The anointing with oil symbolizes their need for God's help and strength so that, undeterred by the bonds of the past and overcoming the opposition of the devil, they will forthrightly take the step of professing their faith and will hold fast to it unfalteringly throughout their lives" (par. 99).

Reflection In the daily newspaper you can read about one person who donates a kidney to save another person. Before some people die, they will their vital organs—liver, heart, lungs—to other people in the hope of preserving some lives. Going to the local blood bank and donating a pint of blood is another way you give the gift of life.

Such an act takes courage. It is a difficult decision to reach. It requires that the donor recognize the good of the recipient. In a sense, the donor is willing to die a little—or a lot!—in exchange for the life of another.

If one person is willing to do this for another person, who is judged to be somewhat just, good or deserving, how much more did God show immense love for everyone through the death of Jesus. Jesus did not die just a little; he was crucified for all people, who are sinners.

Yes, all people are sinners. We are capable and active sinners. There is no one who can raise a hand and declare that he or she is all-just or all-good or even deserving of God's love, demonstrated in Christ's death. But it is precisely in this act of love that Christ died for us and justified us through his own blood.

You are anointed with oil meant to strengthen you in your willingness to give your life away to others and God. This step is a difficult one, for most people prefer to be in charge of their own lives. They prefer to call the shots and make their own decisions. Most people live with the presupposition that their lives are theirs.

You have learned that this presupposition is false. The life of a Christian belongs to God. When a person establishes himself or herself as lord of life, then God's act of love in Jesus goes unheeded. Jesus died for us to show us how to die to self and to live for others and God.

Just as it is with difficulty that a person die a little for a just, good or deserving person, and it is only with courage that he or she does so, Jesus died for us, who are not just, good or deserving. But this is how he showed God's love for us. This is how he showed us what we must be willing to do for each other.

Meditation When have you most recently been willing to die a little for another? To what did you die? By doing so what did you declare just, good or deserving in the other?

Prayer God of love, you proved your love for all people through the self-sacrifice of your Son. On a cross he died for all sinful people and showed them how to be willing to die for each other. Help me to recognize the justice and goodness in every person I meet. Anoint me with the courage to be willing to die a little in order to uphold the dignity of others. Anoint me with the strength to profess my faith in you.

Journal During the week search through the daily newspaper and clip three articles about people who have had the courage to share their lives with others. Identify for each what was shared. Identify for each how the donor declared the recipient just, good or deserving.

The Search

Scripture "A woman of Samaria came to draw water. Jesus said to her, 'Give me a drink....' The Samaritan woman said to him, 'How can you, a Jew, ask me, a Samaritan woman, for a drink?' (For Jews use nothing in common with Samaritans.) Jesus answered and said to her, 'If you knew the gift of God and who is saying to you, "Give me a drink," you would have asked him and he would have given you living water.' [The woman] said to him, 'Sir, you do not even have a bucket and the cistern is deep; where then can you get this living water?...' Jesus answered and said to her, 'Everyone who drinks this water will be thirsty again; but whoever drinks the water I shall give will never thirst; the water I shall give will become in him [or her] a spring of water welling up to eternal life' " (John 4:7-11, 13-14).

RCIA "The scrutinies...are rites for self-searching and repentance and have above all a spiritual purpose. The scrutinies are meant to uncover, then heal all that is weak, defective, or sinful in the hearts of the elect..." (par. 141).

"...[F]irst of all, the elect are instructed gradually about the mystery of sin, from which the whole world and every person longs to be delivered and thus saved from its present and future consequences. Second, their spirit is filled with Christ the Redeemer, who is the living water (gospel of the Samaritan woman in the first scrutiny)..." (par. 143).

Reflection People in a desert search for water, which ensures their lives. Likewise, people in the world search through the experiences of their lives and the collective experience of the human community in an effort to ensure the meaning of, or the purpose of, their lives. They often characterize this search as a hunger or a thirst which cannot be satisfied.

Some people make their first stop on the pilgrimage of life at the well of drugs. This may occur while they are still in elementary school or in junior high school. Drugs offer the promise of a momentary high and consequent escape from the problems that haunt a young person. Drinking deeply of drugs, the individual hopes for an insight or an understanding of his or her life.

The next well from which one may drink is alcohol. A few beers on Friday night quickly turns into some hard stuff from the family liquor cabinet. First, it is the buzz which makes a person feel good. Second, it is the uncontrolled freedom which supposedly enables a person to be himself or herself before the last flash of light and passing out in a drunken stupor. Like drugs, alcohol is supposed to unveil the meaning of life.

The well of sex is often a stopping place for people in their search for the meaning of life. The desire for an intimate relationship is a thirst which cannot be slaked except by hopping into bed with someone. It is the solution which can be viewed daily on the television soap operas or in movie theaters. Premarital, extramarital and nonmarital sexual relationships represent an attempt to drink deeply of the meaning of life.

However, as we sooner or later come to realize, only one person can offer the water that quenches our thirst for ever: Jesus. Yes, Jesus is the water for which we never thirst again. In fact, one drink from the well of Jesus and we become a gushing fountain understanding the meaning, and the purpose, of life. More, we begin to overflow to eternal life.

You must drink deeply from Jesus' well. You must consume the Scriptures, absorb the doctrine of the Church and imbibe the ways of Jesus. Gradually, as the search continues, you begin to realize your thirst is being slaked and the real meaning, and purpose, of life is being revealed. You are drinking of the living water of the Redeemer.

Meditation Which of your particular thirsts has been slaked through your participation in the catechumenate? How was this accomplished? How has this changed your understanding of the meaning, and purpose, of your life?

Prayer God, for whom we search, your Son, Jesus, offered the water of eternal life from his well to the woman of Samaria as she came to believe in him and to understand the meaning of, and purpose of, her life. Once she drank deeply, she ran off to tell others about this thirst-satisfying water. Keep me close to the well of the living water of Jesus. When I stray, call me back. When I fail, strengthen me with your grace. Guide me in my search and unveil for me the meaning of, and the purpose of, my life.

Journal Make a list of all the wells at which you have stopped to drink during your life. What did you find at each?

Presentation of the Creed
(Third Week of Lent)

Creeds

Scripture "...I handed on to you as of first importance what I also received: that Christ died for our sins in accordance with the scriptures; that he was buried; that he was raised on the third day in accordance with the scriptures; that he appeared to Kephas, then to the Twelve. After that, he appeared to more than five hundred brothers at once, most of whom are still living, though some have fallen asleep. After that he appeared to James, then to all the apostles. Last of all, as one born abnormally, he appeared to me" (1 Corinthians 15:3-8).

RCIA "...[T]he celebrant explains in the homily the meaning and importance of the Creed in relation to the teaching that the elect have already received and to the profession of faith that they must make at their baptism and uphold throughout their lives" (par. 159).

Reflection A creed is a set of fundamental beliefs. Whether you are aware of it or not, you live by a personal creed. Your individual creed might include such beliefs as an apple a day keeps the doctor away; streets should be crossed only on crosswalks at intersections; before food is prepared or eaten your hands must be washed with soap and water; and the yard must be mowed every Saturday.

Most of the time, elements such as these are never written down. However, they function together as a creed, a guide throughout your life. You abide by the principal beliefs in your creed and feel guilty if any one of these is violated.

A religious creed is also a set of fundamental religious beliefs. It is usually written. It is the authoritative formula of a particular community of people. In other words, the community creed expresses in a written formula what the members of the community believe collectively. Furthermore, it guides the lives of the members of the community.

In his first letter to the Corinthians, Paul presents a creed. It is a summary statement of the gospel Paul has preached to the Christian community in Corinth. The members of the community believe that Christ died for their sins, after which he was buried and raised on the third day; then, he appeared to various people. For Paul and the Corinthians, this creed is the basis of their faith as a community. It guides them and keeps them united as a Christian community.

The Church is heir to two creeds—one, the Apostles' Creed, is a written formula that comes from the early Church; the other, the Nicene Creed, is a product of the first three hundred and fifty years of Christianity's attempt to put in written formula the trinitarian faith (the belief that God is one God yet three persons—Father, Son, Spirit) of the members of the Church. Each of these creeds is like a treasure chest, which needs to be opened and carefully explored.

Numerous books have been written on the development of the creeds and the meaning of each of their statements. It is imperative that you who seek the sacraments of initiation understand these professions of faith, as you will be called upon before baptism to state publicly the faith of the Church. Thereafter, you will stand in the midst of the Christian community and recite one of the creeds with the entire Church as the authoritative formula of religious belief and guide for your life.

Meditation   After studying both the Apostles' Creed and the Nicene Creed, which single statement from each of them do you find most enlightening, most confusing? Why? (A copy of both creeds can be found in most missalettes or worship aids in church.)

Prayer   Almighty God, creator of heaven and earth, in order to reconcile all of humanity to yourself, you sent your only-begotten Son, Jesus, to show us how to live. He died for our sins and he was buried. But your Spirit breathed new life into him and raised him from the dead. Enlighten my mind that I might understand the mysteries of your great deeds. Enable me to receive your truths with a sincere heart. And keep me faithful to the new way of life I have chosen.

Journal   Make a list of the articles of your personal religious creed, those guidelines by which you live. Which of these articles are similar to articles found in the Apostles' Creed or the Nicene Creed? Which of these articles need to be changed to conform to the life of the Christian community?

Second Scrutiny
(Fourth Sunday of Lent: Cycle A)

Choices

Scripture   "The LORD said to Samuel: '...Fill your horn with oil, and be on your way. I am sending you to Jesse of Bethlehem, for I have chosen my king from among his sons.'

"...The LORD said to Samuel: 'Do not judge from his appearance or from his lofty stature, because I have rejected him. Not as man sees does God see, because man sees the appearance but the LORD looks into the heart.'

"...Jesse presented seven sons before Samuel, but Samuel said to Jesse, 'The LORD has not chosen any one of these.' Then Samuel asked Jesse, 'Are these all the sons you have?' Jesse replied, 'There is still the youngest, who is tending the sheep.'

"...He was ruddy, a youth handsome to behold and making a splendid appearance. The LORD said, 'There—anoint him, for this is he!' Then Samuel, with the horn of oil in hand, anointed him in the midst of his brothers; and from that day on, the spirit of the LORD rushed upon David" (1 Samuel 16:1, 7, 10-13).

RCIA "The anointing [of catechumens] ordinarily takes place after the homily in a celebration of the word of God, and is conferred on each of the catechumens; this rite of anointing may be celebrated several times during the course of the catechumenate" (par. 100).

Reflection Every day you have to make choices. When you get up in the morning, you choose what to wear. Then, you choose what to eat for breakfast. Once at work, you choose what to do first. You choose cars, doctors and lawyers. You choose to shop at wholesale stores, department stores, discount stores.

When meeting a person for the first time, you choose to relate to another based on that person's appearance. It is a fact of life you will relate in different ways to another who is dressed in a coat and tie and one who is wearing shorts and a tank top. The person dressed in a swimsuit gets a different reaction from you than the one clothed in a business suit.

Even though you may often deny it, you make choices about other people based on appearance: makeup, clothes, hairstyle and body build. There is an unconscious presupposition at work that the way a person looks and what a person wears reveal who that person is.

However, God does not choose people on appearance. The first book of Samuel makes this clear: God's criterion is what is in a person's heart. The heart, the center of the body's life, the seat of emotions, the metaphor for love is God's criterion.

Using this criterion, God chose David to be the king of the Israelites. Even though David was young and nothing other than a shepherd-boy, his heart was set on God. His love was for God. And so Samuel anointed him with the horn of oil to signify that he was the person God had chosen. Upon David God poured out the Spirit, who strengthened David, even when he sinned, to be the best of Israel's kings.

You are anointed with oil in order to strengthen you during your period of preparation for the sacraments of initiation. The oil of catechumens is smeared on your forehead as a sign that God is pleased with what God sees in your heart. God has chosen you to follow in the pathways of Jesus.

Once you are baptized, you are anointed with the chrism oil, a sweet-smelling perfume. This post-baptismal anointing, confirmation, is another sign of God's choice. Sealed with oil as priests, prophets and kings, God strengthens you to continue your pilgrimage of faith.

When you are ill, you are anointed with the oil of the sick. This ointment is meant to strengthen you in suffering. The Spirit is sent as a comforter and consoler, another sign of God's choice of you.

Just as you make choices every day, so too does God make a choice to strengthen you through the anointing with oil. God sees what is in your heart. God chooses you. Then God strengthens you with the Spirit.

Meditation In the past hour, what choices have you made? How were you anointed with the strength of the Spirit to persevere in each of your choices?

Prayer Lord, you sent your servant, Samuel, to anoint David, son of Jesse, as king of your people Israel. With the horn of oil in his hand he found the man whose heart you had judged worthy of your special gift. Be with me and guide me as I make choices every day. Purify my heart that I might seek to do your will. Remove the blindness of appearance that keeps me from seeing you in the faces of all whom I meet. Anoint me with the gift of the Spirit.

Journal What do you consider to be the three toughest choices of your life? For each identify who strengthened you or anointed you. For each identify what appearance you had to see through in order to get to the heart of the matter.

Light

Scripture "...[Y]ou were once darkness, but now you are light in the Lord. Live as children of light, for light produces every kind of goodness and righteousness and truth.... Take no part in the fruitless works of darkness; ...everything exposed by the light becomes visible, for everything that becomes visible is light. Therefore, it says:

> 'Awake, O sleeper,
> and arise from the dead,
> and Christ will give you light' " (Ephesians 5:8-9, 11, 13-14).

RCIA "At the celebrations belonging to the period of the catechumenate, the faithful should seek to be present whenever possible and should take an active part in the responses, prayers, singing, and acclamations" (par. 9:2).

"On the day of election, because it is a day of growth for the community, the faithful, when called upon, should be sure to give honest and carefully considered testimony about the catechumens" (par. 9:3).

Reflection The daily rhythms of day and night become so much a part of your life they go unnoticed most of the time. Yet, it is these very daily rhythms which dictate so much of your life. The first rays of the dawn indicate it is time to wake up and rise from sleep; a new day for work or play begins. At midday the overhead sun indicates half the day is spent; some work or play must be finished quickly or put off until the next day. When evening comes, the setting sun and encroaching darkness indicate a period of rest. The deep darkness of night tells you it is time to go to bed and sleep and rejuvenate the body for the new day, which will peek over the horizon in a few hours.

Within this daily rhythm, you attempt to follow Jesus. The pilgrimage of faith with Jesus is made primarily in the light, which comes from those who are fellow travelers. Thus, by their bodily presence and their active participation in liturgical prayer, the faithful shine in the darkness and light the way for you who seek the sacraments of initiation.

However, you are not without light. You too bring a new brightness to the community of believers. As your light continues to increase, you help build up the Church; you cause growth to take place throughout the whole community. Every time a new catechumen is admitted into the community, the whole Church glows with a little more light.

This truth is acted out in symbol on Holy Saturday during the Easter Vigil with two services of light. The first begins outside, where a new fire is kindled in the darkness of the night. From this fire the Easter Candle is kindled and proclaimed to be a sign of the risen Christ, as it leads the procession of faithful and elect into the dark church. The faithful carry candles lighted from the Easter Candle. The Church comes aglow with the light of Christ in the midst of the light of his faithful followers.

After you are baptized, you, the elect-become-neophytes (the newly baptized), are given candles lit from the Easter Candle. You are told you have been enlightened by Christ and you are to walk always as a child of the light. The flame represents not only your newly risen status, but also your faith, which needs to be kept alive in your heart.

Before you came to believe, you were in darkness, asleep as it were. Now, however, through immersion into the paschal mystery—the death and resurrection of Jesus—you have been awakened and told to arise from the dead. The risen Christ now gives you light, which you are to let shine so that others might find the way as you have.

Once you have received your lighted candle, all members of the Easter Vigil community re-ignite their candles from the Easter Candle and, in your presence, renew their baptismal promises. Through fasting, prayer, almsgiving and self-sacrifice, the entire community has died to sin during Lent. Now, it is awakened to the light of a renewed life. The Church is filled with light. Every year hereafter, you will join in this rhythm of darkness and light.

Meditation When have you most recently functioned as light for someone? What was the occasion? How did you receive light from the person to whom you offered it?

Prayer God of light, you have made us children of your light and you produce within us every kind of goodness, righteousness and truth. Instill in my heart the knowledge of what is pleasing to you. Enable me to let my light shine that others might find the way. Help me to trust in your promise that one day you will awaken me from the sleep of death to live forever in eternal light with Jesus.

Journal Identify the three major occasions in your life when someone shared some light with you. What light was shed upon you? In return what light did you share with the other person?

Sight

Scripture "...Jesus...said, 'Do you believe in the Son of Man?' (The man who had been blind from birth but could now see) answered and said, 'Who is he, sir, that I may believe in him?' Jesus said to him, 'You have seen him and the one speaking with you is he.' He said, 'I do believe, Lord,' and he worshiped him. Then Jesus said, 'I came into this world for judgment, so that those who do not see might see, and those who do see might become blind' " (John 9:35-39).

RCIA "...[T]he scrutinies are celebrated in order to deliver the elect from the power of sin and Satan, to protect them against temptation, and to give them strength in Christ, who is the way, the truth, and the life" (par. 141).

"...[T]he elect are instructed gradually about the mystery of sin .... [T]heir spirit is filled with Christ the Redeemer, who is...the light of the world (gospel of the man born blind in the second scrutiny)..." (par. 143).

Reflection In many instances when you say, "I see," you are employing the sense of sight as a metaphor. After the boss explains to you how the job should be done, you say, "I see." What you mean is that you understand the directions, which have been given by the boss.

In attempting to understand the directions in a computer manual, one coworker tells you, "Oh, I see." What had not been understood before becomes perfectly clear with a little help, instruction or demonstration from you who already see.

You do not take literally the question, "Do you see what I'm talking about?" during a serious conversation. The metaphor of sight is being compared to the clear reception of ideas and information.

In John's Gospel seeing is a metaphor for faith. Those who can see are those who believe in Jesus. The irony found in the account of the man born blind is not found in the restoration of his physical sight, but in his gradual coming to faith. Step-by-step through the story the man's eyes are opened until he makes a profession of faith in the Son of Man and worships Jesus.

He is contrasted to the other characters in the story, who supposedly think that they see, when in fact they are blind. Yes, they see physically, but they do not believe. Only the blind man can see! Those who can see are blind!

The Johannine Jesus is portrayed as a judge, who permits

people to see themselves as they really are. He does not render judgment directly; people judge themselves based on whether or not they have faith in Jesus. Those who see are often trapped in their own sight; they see only what they want to see. Those who are blind are free to see without limits.

You are a person who knows that you were once blind and are slowly beginning to see. You realize your faith will always need a little clearer focus as you make your lifetime journey with the whole Church. Jesus is recognized as the light of the world, who invites only those who are blind to see. Those who see have no need for sight!

Meditation What Scripture story, teaching of the Church or idea are you having the most difficulty seeing right now?

Prayer God of light, when the darkness of sin had covered the world, you sent the Son of Man to spread your light. To the blind he offered the gift of sight; to the seeing he revealed their own judgment on themselves. Open my eyes that I might see the signs of your presence in the wonders of creation. Open my eyes that I might recognize you in my brothers and sisters. Strengthen my faith in the light of the world, your Son, the Lord Jesus Christ.

Journal With what have you most recently been blinded? How has someone restored your sight? Who helped you? How did this person help? In what situation have you found yourself seeing and being able to help another see? Why did you help? How did you help?

Third Scrutiny
(Fifth Sunday of Lent: Cycle A)

Buried

Scripture "Thus says the Lord God: O my people, I will open your graves and have you rise from them, and bring you back to the land of Israel. Then you shall know that I am the Lord, when I open your graves and have you rise from them, O my people! I will put my spirit in you that you may live..." (Ezekiel 37:12-14).

RCIA "During Lent, the period of purification and enlightenment, the faithful should take care to participate in the rites of the scrutinies and presentations and give the elect the example of their own renewal in the spirit of penance, faith, and charity. At the Easter Vigil, they should attach great importance to renewing their own baptismal promises" (par. 9:4).

Reflection When you hear the word "bury," you probably think about a dead person. The dead are buried; burial is one acceptable way of disposing of the remains of someone who has died. The body of the deceased is lowered into a hole in the earth and covered over. Thus, the dead one is buried.

However, "bury" is also used to describe being hidden from view. For example, a bill is buried in a stack of papers. A dog buries a bone in the backyard. You bury your face in your hands when you are ashamed of something you've done.

"Bury" is used to describe being overloaded with work. A secretary is buried in paperwork. A business manager is buried in employee disputes or union talks. Worries often bury parents as they raise their children.

Life can be aptly described as a series of burials and

resurrections to new life. However, the primary focus is not on the burial but on what follows it.

Lent is a time set aside for climbing out of your grave. During Lent you are purified and enlightened; you are called forth from your self-made grave to share in the new life of the Church. The faithful spend Lent looking at the graves they have dug for themselves since the previous Lent. They are called to come forth and prepare to renew their baptismal promises during the Easter Vigil through their acts of penance, faith and charity.

The motivation for coming forth from your grave is the promise of God to breathe new life into you. God calls you from the grave with the word. God directs you with light. God washes away the grime of the grave with baptism and anoints your body with the sweet-smelling oil of the Holy Spirit. You are fed with the bread from heaven and you drink from the cup of salvation.

The going into the grave is an experience of life. Throughout your life, you get into the grave. This is in practice for the final time, when you will make your last great act of trust. Just as God has called you from the grave so many times during your life, so your final act of trust in God is that God will call you forth again to eternal life.

You prepare for your first call from the grave, which will take place in baptism. On Holy Saturday evening you will be immersed into the watery tomb, from which you will be born again and arise as God's new creation. You will be immersed into the paschal mystery—a lifetime of dying and rising with Christ.

The faithful will eagerly renew the promises which they made when they were baptized. They will remember the many times since baptism when they have gone into the grave and been called forth. Together, you and the faithful share the experiences of burial and being called out of the grave by God.

Meditation What has been your most recent experience of being buried? Who helped you out of the grave?

Prayer God of the tomb, when your people felt like they were dead in their captivity, you sent your prophet Ezekiel to proclaim new life to them. You called them forth from their graves and breathed your Spirit into them. As I continue my pilgrimage of faith, speak your word of new life to me. Through my Lenten discipline, open the grave I have dug and raise me from it. Breathe into me the gift of the Spirit and bring me back to faithfulness. Help me to know you.

Journal What are your three major experiences of being buried and raised to new life in your journey of faith? Identify for each who helped you out of your grave. Identify one person whom you have helped out of the grave. What was the grave that person was in? How did you help?

Paschal Mystery

Scripture "...[Y]ou are in the spirit, if only the Spirit of God dwells in you. Whoever does not have the Spirit of Christ does not belong to him. But if Christ is in you, although the body is dead because of sin, the spirit is alive because of righteousness. If the Spirit of the one who raised Jesus from the dead dwells in you, the one who raised Christ from the dead will give life to your mortal bodies also, through his Spirit that dwells in you" (Romans 8:9-11).

RCIA "The third step in the Christian initiation of adults is the celebration of the sacraments of baptism, confirmation, and eucharist. Through this final step the elect, receiving pardon for their sins, are admitted into the people of God" (par. 206).
"The usual time for the celebration of the sacraments of initiation is the Easter Vigil..." (par. 207).

Reflection The sacraments of initiation—Baptism, Confirmation, Eucharist—are best celebrated at the annual

Easter Vigil because of the connection between these sacraments and the death and resurrection of Christ. All three sacraments of initiation involve dying and being raised in fulfillment of God's promise.

Baptism is the sacrament of death and new birth. You are immersed, drowned, in the Spirit-filled death-dealing watery tomb. Then, you are born again as you are raised up from the tomb that has become a womb. The first trace of the paschal mystery—the death and resurrection of Jesus—is made on your life.

Through the postbaptismal anointing you are sealed with the special gifts of the Holy Spirit. Confirmation is a death to possession or ownership of your personal gifts. Dying to self, you, the newly baptized, rise to a new understanding that your special gift or talent is for the good of the community in order to build the Church. The Spirit gives gifts to individual persons to be used for all.

The Eucharist is a celebration of death and resurrection. Not only is the death and resurrection of Jesus recalled, but we recall all the times we have died since baptism and all the times God has brought us to new life. Just as many grains of wheat are ground to make flour which rises up as bread, so do we die to ourselves and rise to that unity which is the Church. Likewise, just as many individual grapes are crushed and fermented into one cup of wine, so many different people put to death their own desires and rise as a community on a pilgrimage of faith.

The celebration of the sacraments of initiation is the culmination of all past experiences of washing, anointing and feeding others as well as all past experience of being washed, anointed and fed by others. Indeed, daily washing, perfuming and eating serve as reminders of the great Easter Vigil event.

You wash others with a kind word, advice, a demonstration of care. You anoint others with providing a shoulder to cry on, a hug, a kiss or simple presence. You feed others with a surprise invitation to lunch or dinner or with an unexpected gift. All of these are special moments that connect people to the paschal mystery. By being willing to embrace death, life is found. God is faithful to the promise that death does not end in death, but always ends in new life.

Meditation Who has most recently washed you, anointed you, fed you? How were you washed, anointed and fed? Who have you most recently washed, anointed, fed? How did you wash, anoint and feed that person?

Prayer God, through the suffering, death and resurrection of your Son you have established the paschal mystery. Baptize me into your Spirit. Seal me with your special gifts. Feed me with the body and blood of Christ. Instill in me your Spirit, who raised Jesus from the dead, that I might always trust your promise to raise me from the dead through this same Spirit. Make me worthy of my initiation into the paschal mystery of the Lord Jesus Christ.

Journal What is the major experience of your life of being washed by another, being anointed by another, being fed by another? Identify the ways each of these was a sharing in the paschal mystery. In other words, to what did you die and what new life did you discover?

Eternal Life

Scripture "Martha said to Jesus, 'Lord, if you had been here, my brother would not have died. (But) even now I know that whatever you ask of God, God will give you.' Jesus said to her, 'Your brother will rise.' Martha said to him, 'I know he will rise, in the resurrection on the last day.' Jesus told her, 'I am the resurrection and the life; whoever believes in me, even if he [or she] dies, will live, and everyone who lives and believes in me will never die. Do you believe this?' She said to him, 'Yes, Lord. I have come to believe that you are the Messiah, the Son of God, the one who is coming into the world' " (John 11:21-27).

RCIA "[The scrutinies]...should complete the conversion of the elect and deepen their resolve to hold fast to Christ and to carry out their decision to love God above all" (par. 141).

"...The elect are instructed gradually about the mystery of sin.... [T]heir spirit is filled with Christ the Redeemer, who is...the resurrection and the life (gospel of Lazarus in the third scrutiny). From the first to the final scrutiny the elect should progress in their perception of sin and their desire for salvation" (par. 143).

Reflection Today, society in general possesses a great fear of death. For the most part, the dying are confined to nursing homes or hospital beds; seldom does anyone die at home anymore, unless it is an accident or there was no time to get the person to the hospital. Thus, death is hidden from the public eye.

When a person does finally die, no one dares to say, "He is dead." The fear of death is clothed in such phrases as, "He has passed away" or "She has fallen asleep" or "How natural and peaceful he or she looks!" Talking about death in terms of finality of earthly existence scares us because we are reminded of our own inevitable deaths. Indeed, countless death and dying books have been written and courses are offered to help us cope with the reality of the death of others and the fact that some day everyone must die.

You who believe in Jesus, the resurrection and the life, should have no fear of death. To you, death is not the end of life; it is but a passageway from one form of life to another. Your day of baptism is your birthday into eternal life. It removes the finality of death. You continue to live after death in a different and eternal form.

Death is your final opportunity to profess your faith in God. It is your last chance to trust the God who permitted his own Son to die and then raised him to eternal life. God has already demonstrated that God is worthy of trust and keeps the promises that have been made. Jesus is the living reminder. What happened to Jesus—death—will happen to you. What happened to Jesus—resurrection to eternal life—will happen to you who believe that he is the Messiah, the Son of God.

Jesus' gift to the world is freedom from the fear of death. In fact, you should be willing to embrace death, hug it intimately and name it for what it is. It is but another step in the earthly lifetime and eternal lifetime journey of salvation.

Meditation What is your greatest fear about death? What do you need to do in order to eliminate this fear? How can other believers help you eliminate your fear of death?

Prayer God of the resurrection, when sin and death entered the world, you sent your Son to offer the gift of eternal life. You permitted him to suffer the agony and death of the cross, but you would not permit him to sleep in death. On the third day, you raised him to new life. Help me to acknowledge my fear of death. Deepen my resolve to hold fast to Jesus, the resurrection and the life. Make me eager to share with him in the new life of the kingdom.

Journal Make a list of the people you have known who have died. As far as you know, how did their faith strengthen them to face death?

Presentation of the Lord's Prayer
(Fifth Week of Lent)

Abba, Father

Scripture "As proof that you are children, God sent the spirit of his Son into our hearts, crying out, 'Abba, Father!' So you are no longer a slave but a child, and if a child then also an heir, through God" (Galatians 4:6-7).

RCIA "The presentation of the Lord's Prayer...should preferably be celebrated in the presence of a community of the faithful, within Mass" (par. 178).

"After the gospel presentation, the celebrant in the homily explains the meaning and importance of the Lord's Prayer" (par. 181).

Reflection You know that God is neither male nor female, and that it is just as appropriate to call God "Mother" as it is to call God "Father." However, the scriptural designation of God as "Father" reflects a patriarchal society in which men were dominant and objects of honor, while women were passive and objects of shame. Also, you will note that calling God either "Father" or "Mother" is predicating human language and human names for the Divine, who is beyond all speech and without name.

Jesus called God "Abba" ("Daddy"), which indicated a filial intimacy. Naming God "Abba" was a radical move on the part of Jesus. By employing this name for God, Jesus made the unnamed God of Israel available to people. This term of endearment indicates that God cares for us, like a father cares for his son, his heir—in a patriarchal society.

In his Letter to the Galatians, Paul explains that God has made us his children through the work of the Spirit. At one time we thought of ourselves as slaves to God's law; now, we think of ourselves as free, adopted children, brothers and sisters of Jesus and heirs to everything that God owns.

You can call upon God as "Mother." Certainly God has brought you to birth and nurtured your life while you were still hidden in your mother's womb. God offers her breast of grace from which you may suckle. God fosters independence, healing and forgiveness during your early growing years. Like a mother, there is nothing God will not do for you.

In order to fuse the complimentary image of "Father" and "Mother," you may prefer to call God "Parent." This designation connotes both the male and female aspects of

God's care for you. Whatever name you use for God, you should remember that naming is something human beings do. When all is said and done, there is no name that can adequately describe the God who has made all people children of God and heirs of God's kingdom.

Therefore, when you come together with others, you need to agree upon a name for God, knowing that no name adequately implies exactly who God is. As a community of believers, one individual joins with many others, and together all remember they are adopted children. All are equal heirs of eternal life which flows from the death and resurrection of Jesus, the unique Son of God.

Meditation What is your favorite name for God? What are the implications of this name for God?

Prayer Our Father, who art in heaven, hallowed be your name; your kingdom come; your will be done on earth as it is in heaven. Give us this day our daily bread and forgive us our trespasses as we forgive those who trespass against us; and lead us not into temptation, but deliver us from evil.

Journal Make a list of as many names for God as you can. You may want to search the Bible for names for God. What does each name imply about God?

Chapter Four

Preparation Rites on Holy Saturday

"When it is possible to bring the elect together on Holy Saturday for reflection and prayer, some or all of the following rites may be celebrated as an immediate preparation for the sacraments: the presentation of the Lord's Prayer, if it has been deferred, the "return" or recitation of the Creed, the ephphetha rite, the choosing of a baptismal name" (*RCIA*, par. 185:2).

Recitation of the Creed

Who Are You?

Scripture "When Jesus went into the region of Caesarea Philippi he asked his disciples, 'Who do people say that the Son of Man is?' They replied, 'Some say John the Baptist, others Elijah, still others Jeremiah or one of the prophets.' He said to them, 'But who do you say that I am?' " (Matthew 16:13-15).

RCIA "The rite of recitation of the Creed prepares the elect for the profession of faith they will make immediately before they are baptized...; the rite also instructs them in their duty to proclaim the message of the Gospel" (par. 193).

Reflection The first bit of information you receive about a person to whom you are being introduced is the other person's name. Once another person's name is firmly etched in your mind, the next question two people usually ask each other is, "What do you do?" This question implies occupation. John might say, "I am a teacher." Mary replies, "I used to be a teacher, but now I am a sales representative." With teacher being common ground, the two people can launch into a more detailed conversation.

Your name and occupation disclose information about you. As you learn another's name and the type of work the other does, you are forming an image of who the person is. Gradually, you reach a preliminary understanding of the personality, emotional stability and range of experience of the other.

There are various names given to Jesus; each of these names reveals some aspect of the meaning of Jesus. Each name used for Jesus indicates something about him. The various names of Jesus are like a window through which you can see him; however, each name provides a different perspective or angle from which you view Jesus.

Among other meanings, to call Jesus the "Son of Man" is to see him as a human being. It is a title which expresses the fact that Jesus was a person like everyone else. "Son of Man" is a designation of Jesus' fully human status.

The title "Messiah" refers to Jesus as the "anointed one." In Judaism there was an expectation of the appearance of a descendant of David, who would restore Roman-dominated Israel to the glory of the days of the Davidic rule. This political ruler would be the "anointed one," the person chosen by God, like David was chosen by God and anointed with oil by Samuel. In Greek "Messiah" is translated as "Christ."

To declare Jesus the "Son of the living God," as Matthew uniquely portrays Peter doing, is to make a post-resurrectional confession of faith. This title focuses on the divinity of Jesus, the One whom God raised from the dead, the righteous One of God.

The very name "Jesus" is a declaration. In Hebrew the name is Joshua; it means "Yahweh saves" or "Yahweh helps." Yahweh, the name for God that God gave to Moses, refers to the saving aspect of Jesus' life, death and resurrection. He rescued us from sin and removed the alienation that existed between us and God. In other words, Jesus saved the world.

Matthew, in narrating the birth of Jesus, tells us that Jesus is "Emmanuel." This title, borrowed from the prophet Isaiah, means "God is with us." It refers to the everlasting presence of God and his risen Son with us. Only Matthew's Gospel ends with Jesus' promise to be with people until the end of the age.

Luke prefers to call Jesus "Lord." This title, frequently applied to Yahweh or God in the Old Testament, refers to Jesus' transcendence and dominion over the whole world. It is a post-resurrectional confession of faith.

Meditation What is your favorite title or name for Jesus? Why? What does this title reveal to you about Jesus?

Prayer Father, you have revealed to your people your only-begotten Son, whom they call the Son of Man, the Messiah, the Lord. Open my eyes to see the humanity of the Son of Man. Open my mind to understand the wisdom of the Savior. Open my heart to the love of Emmanuel. Anoint me with your strength that I might profess you as the one and eternal God—Father, Son and Holy Spirit.

Journal Choose three titles of Jesus from those listed above. Search through the New Testament until you find each title used once. Make a notation of where you found the title and how it is used. What view does the story, in which the title is used, give you of Jesus?

Ephphetha Rite

Openings

Scripture "...[P]eople brought to [Jesus] a deaf man who had a speech impediment and begged him to lay his hand on him. He took him off by himself away from the crowd. He put his finger into the man's ears and, spitting, touched his tongue; then he looked up to heaven and groaned, and said to him, '*Ephphatha*!' (that is, 'Be opened!') And [immediately] the man's ears were opened, his speech impediment was removed, and he spoke plainly" (Mark 7:32-35).

RCIA "By the power of its symbolism the ephphetha rite, or rite of opening the ears and mouth, impresses on the elect their need of grace in order that they may hear the word of God and profess it for their salvation" (par. 197).

Reflection Many openings take place during your lifetime. The first few years of your childhood were a never-ending series of new openings. As a child you discovered your fingers and toes. Then, you found other people and toys. After learning how to walk, you looked for anything that could be held in your hand and put into your mouth.

Your first day of school was an opening. The school building was an open door to new ideas, new discipline, new friends. Also, every school year was a new opening, as you progressed through learning how to drive in high school to making decisions that would affect your life in college or the work world.

Another new opening occurs on the day of marriage. Two people mutually open their lives to each other and face the unknown together. They promise nothing less than to join together in facing all the new openings that will come their way. Perhaps in the future, the couple will experience another new opening in the birth of their firstborn child.

Just as your lifetime is a succession of new openings, so is your faith a succession of new openings to the grace of God. With all the daily noise from television, radio and others, it is easy not to hear the word of God. Therefore, your ears have to be opened always. Then, God can speak in the quiet of your heart and direct your life.

Likewise, it is easy not to speak the word of God. Therefore, your speech impediment has to be removed. Then, you can speak from the inner depths of your solitude about the mystery of God's grace.

To stand opened does leave you vulnerable to any experience. However, it is the stance God requests. God's free gift of grace can only flow into you if you are open, willing to bend.

Meditation What needs to be opened in your life? What fears do you have about this opening?

Prayer God of grace, through your Son, Jesus, you opened the ears of the deaf, you loosed the tongues of the mute and you poured out your grace to those who would accept your free gift. Open my ears to hear you in every sound of the day. Loose my tongue to sing your praise in every word I speak. Enable me to be a bearer of the good news of salvation.

Journal Make a list of the openings that have occurred in your life in the past three months. How was God at work in each opening?

Chapter Five

Celebration of the Sacraments of Initiation (Easter Vigil)

"The third step: having completed their spiritual preparation, [the elect] receive the sacraments of Christian initiation" (*RCIA*, par. 6:3).

Creation: God's Work

Scripture "In the beginning, when God created the heavens and the earth, the earth was a formless wasteland, and darkness covered the abyss, while a mighty wind swept over the waters....

"Then God said: 'Let us make man in our image, after our likeness....'

> "God created man in his image;
> in the divine image he created him;
> male and female he created them.

"God looked at everything he had made, and he found it very good.

> "Thus the heavens and the earth and all their array were completed" (Genesis 1:1-2, 26, 27, 31, 2:1).

RCIA "The celebration of baptism begins with the blessing of water.... The blessing...introduces an invocation of the Trinity at the very outset of the celebration of baptism. For it calls to mind the mystery of God's love from the beginning of the world and the creation of the human race; by invoking the Holy Spirit and proclaiming Christ's death and resurrection, it impresses on the mind the newness of Christian baptism, by which we share in his own death and resurrection and receive the holiness of God himself" (par. 210).

Reflection The Book of Genesis in the Bible contains two accounts of creation. You may prefer the second account of creation in which work is viewed as a curse bestowed upon humankind because of the disobedience of the first couple. However, the Bible balances this perspective with the first account of creation in which God is portrayed as the worker.

Out of formlessness and darkness God creates by the power of the wind of God's sweeping word. God needs only to pronounce the word "light" and it becomes reality. God says "the sky" and "the earth" and these immediately spring into being.

However, the summit of God's creation is humankind, man and woman made in the very likeness of God. When you see another human being you view God, since everyone reflects another face of the myriad possibilities that exist in God. Thus, every human being by his or her presence upon the earth reveals another aspect of God to you.

When you engage in work, you engage in the creative energy of God. Since you are made in the image of God, like God you create. Sometimes, in your work you are called a cocreator—you share in God's work.

You share in God's work through the arts. The potter at the wheel shapes and molds the clay, just as God shapes and molds people with his word. The musician carefully crafts the notes of a new composition, as God inspires people to sing praise. The paints the artist brushes are a sharing in the work of God, who splashes the universe with color.

The farmer's work is a sharing in the toil of God, as God feeds people. The one who tills the soil and raises the crop provides for others just as God provides grace for all people. Those who care for the earth and protect the environment attempt to keep the universe in the very good state in which it was created.

The most intimate way you share in the work of God is through the creation of new life. When husband and wife are joined together in the total act of giving themselves to each other, a new life can be conceived. Just as God first created people in his own image and likeness, man and woman continue to procreate others in the same image and likeness.

Baptism initiates you into the greatest of God's works— the raising of Jesus from the dead. Through Jesus' resurrection, God recreated us and bestowed upon every believer the gift of eternal life. Through baptism you share in the death and resurrection of Jesus; that is, you are recreated and given a share in the work of the holiness of the ever-creating God.

Meditation Do you view work as a blessing or a curse? Explain.

Prayer God of work, from the beginning of time you have been creating the heavens and the earth to reveal your presence to your people. The climax of creation was man and woman, made in your own image. Yet, even this was surpassed when you raised your Son, Jesus, from the dead and recreated the human race. Through baptism you give me a share in this new creation. Help me to see in the work of my hands my likeness to yourself.

Journal Make a list of three works you have done today. How is each a sharing in God's creativity?

Faithfulness

Scripture "...God put Abraham to the test. He called to him, 'Abraham!' 'Ready!' he replied. Then God said: 'Take your son Isaac, your only one, whom you love, and go to the land of Moriah. There you shall offer him up as a holocaust on a height that I will point out to you.' Early the next morning Abraham saddled his donkey, took with him his son Isaac, and two of his servants as well, and with the wood that he had cut for the holocaust, set out for the place of which God had told him.

"When they came to the place of which God had told him, Abraham built an altar there and arranged the wood on it. Next he tied up his son Isaac, and put him on top of the wood on the altar. Then he reached out and took the knife to slaughter his son. But the LORD's messenger called to him, from heaven, 'Abraham, Abraham!' 'Yes, Lord,' he answered. 'Do not lay your hand on the boy,' said the messenger. 'Do not do the least thing to him. I know now how devoted you are to God, since you did not withhold from me your own beloved son' " (Genesis 22:1-3, 9-12).

R C I A "Adults are not saved unless they come forward of their own accord and with the will to accept God's gift through their own belief. The faith of those to be baptized is not simply the faith of the Church, but the personal faith of each one of them and each one of them is expected to keep it a living faith" (par. 211).

R e f l e c t i o n Literally, if you are "faithful" you are full of faith. You are steadfast or loyal; you adhere to your promises and you trust that others will do the same. As a faithful person you are determined to adhere to what you believe.

In the Christian tradition, Abraham is an example of a faithful person. He had received the promise from God that his descendants would be as numerous as the stars in the sky or the sands on the seashore. However, he had only one son from his marriage with Sarah. Following what was probably the primitive custom of child-sacrifice of his culture, Abraham believed that God wanted him to offer Isaac as a holocaust.

While the original text of this narrative was most likely used to show God's rejection of the child sacrifice practice of Abraham's time, Christian tradition has focused on Abraham's faithfulness to God. Abraham did not waver; he remained faithful. Even if it made no sense to him how God would give him many descendants if his only heir were offered to God, Abraham was firm in his allegiance to God. The God of Abraham quickly realized how faithful his servant was.

You will find it difficult to remain faithful. In fact, you may find it easier to be faithless than faithful. You who are faithful often suffer ostracization; you may discover you have not been invited to the latest social gathering of the "old group." It is tempting to downplay faith and rejoin the group because social acceptance means so much today. However, if you are faithful, you are willing to stand firm and to demonstrate that your faith is alive.

Your faithfulness is often challenged in the moral arena. Doesn't everyone cheat a little on income taxes? But can you, the faithful person, do this? Must not you demonstrate your loyalty to the principles of truth and honesty?

Faithfulness calls you to adhere to the right to life. Every human being from the moment of conception deserves to be treated with human dignity. When the life of the unborn is threatened, when white supremacy is preached, when the aged are put to death, you, the faithful person, must adhere to the right to life.

You must demonstrate faithfulness in the workplace. Gossip is not being faithful. Getting ahead at any expense in order to get a promotion or a pay raise does not illustrate faithfulness. Your loyalty to your baptismal promises is carried wherever you happen to be. It is not a Sunday-only faithfulness, but one that permeates all of your life; it is a living faithfulness.

Meditation Identify one occasion within the past week when you remained faithful and had to sacrifice something or yourself in order to do so. Also, within the past week, identify one occasion when you did not remain faithful. What were you not willing to sacrifice?

Prayer God of Abraham, you called your servant to take his only-beloved son and present him as a sacrifice. Abraham obeyed your word and demonstrated his faithfulness. In the course of time, you sent your only-begotten Son, Jesus, who preached your word and remained faithful to you to his death on the cross. By raising him from the dead you have revealed you are worthy of my trust. Strengthen my faith in your word. Guide me in giving witness to your truth. Help me to make of my life a living sacrifice.

Journal Identify three major sacrifices you have had to make in your life. To what did you remain faithful? Has God been at work in each sacrifice? How?

Passover

Scripture "...Moses stretched out his hand over the sea, and the LORD swept the sea with a strong east wind throughout the night and so turned it into dry land. When the water was thus divided, the Israelites marched into the midst of the sea on dry land, with the water like a wall to their right and to their left.

"The Egyptians followed in pursuit: all Pharaoh's horses and chariots and charioteers went after them right into the midst of the sea.

"Then the LORD told Moses, 'Stretch out your hand over the sea, that the water may flow back upon the Egyptians, upon their chariots and their charioteers....' As the water flowed back, it covered the chariots and the charioteers of Pharaoh's whole army which had followed the Israelites into the sea. Not a single one of them escaped.... Thus the LORD saved Israel on that day from the power of the Egyptians" (Exodus 14:21-23, 26, 28, 30).

RCIA "The celebration of baptism begins with the blessing of water.... The blessing declares the religious meaning of water as God's creation and the sacramental use of water in the unfolding of the paschal mystery, and the blessing is also a remembrance of God's wonderful works in the history of salvation" (par. 210).

Reflection The Hebrew Scriptures (Old Testament) are filled with remembrances of the events of God's act of saving people. Most of the time these narratives are framed by some type of passing over.

The Hebrews are passed over by the avenging angel because they have smeared the blood of the lamb on their doorposts. The pillar of cloud by day and fire by night, which guides the Hebrews out of Egypt, passes over them when they get to the Sea of Reeds; this protects them from an attack by Pharaoh's army. The people pass over (through) the Sea of Reeds. Later, when Joshua becomes the leader of Israel, he leads the people through (passes over) the Jordan

River into the promised land. In the Elijah and Elisha cycle of stories in the Book of Kings, several "passing overs" are retold.

In every passover the people face death, but they are rescued by God. The history of salvation is nothing other than a string of events of God's constant rescue of people. People pass over from death to life. We refer to this as the paschal mystery.

"Paschal" points back to the remembrance of the passover lamb, whose blood saved the Hebrews. "Mystery" relates the unheard of activity of a God who is ever-willing to rescue people.

The greatest passover of all time was the rescue of Jesus from death. Like the paschal lamb, his blood was spread on the wood of the cross. But as God had rescued those who remained faithful to him so many times in the past, once again God saved; this time God raised Jesus from the dead.

Through baptism you are immersed into the paschal mystery. What happened to Jesus continues to happen to you. Suffering and death are inevitable. However, by remembering the saving events of God throughout history, you realize that nothing can defeat you. God always rescues you.

Meditation When did you most recently experience a passover? What death did you face? What new life did you discover? How did God rescue you?

Prayer God of the passover, you have always demonstrated your love for your people by rescuing them from death. With great signs and wonders you led your chosen people from Egyptian slavery to the land of freedom. With the sign of the cross you led all people from the slavery of sin to the freedom of being your children. Always etch in my memory the great works of salvation as you now prepare me for my passover from death to life in the waters of baptism. Keep me faithful to Jesus, your Son, who has already passed over from death to life.

Journal List the three greatest passovers of your life. Identify for each the death faced and the new life embraced. Also, identify for each how the passover changed you or your perspective on reality.

Come Back

Scripture "The LORD calls you back,
  like a wife forsaken and grieved in spirit,
A wife married in youth and then cast off,
  says your God.
For a brief moment I abandoned you,
  but with great tenderness I will take you back.
In an outburst of wrath, for a moment
  I hid my face from you;
But with enduring love I take pity on you,
  says the LORD, your redeemer"
(Isaiah 54:6-8).

RCIA "[The elect] are graced with adoption as children of God and are led by the Holy Spirit into the promised fullness of time begun in Christ and, as they share in the eucharistic sacrifice and meal, even to a foretaste of the kingdom of God" (par. 206).

Reflection "Come back," one child calls to another, after they have had a fight over toys or how a game should be played or where they will ride their bicycles. "Come back," says a young person to another after the wrong words were said on a date. When one friend leaves the home of another, he or she says, "Come back."

Since most of us do not walk backward, if we accept the invitation to come back, we must turn around and face the individual who issues the call. After a disagreement this may not be easy. After a good time of sharing and fun, coming back is a delight, as we seek to relive the past moments of ecstasy.

God is always calling you to come back. The Lord of all the earth not only issues the invitation, but God says that you are accepted unconditionally. With the tenderness of a mother receiving her child who decided to run away from home, God opens up arms wide and embraces you who come back. Like parents who yearn to have a child of their own, God adopts every person on the earth as God's children.

When you come back to God, the Lord frees you from your slavery of going away. Going away can be slavery to sin. Going away when you are angry with another is nothing other than being a slave to sin; you are being controlled by anger. Going away hurt when a relationship is failing is not dealing with the reasons for the relationship failure; you are being dominated by feelings of being hurt. Likewise, going away when the terms of a business deal are not exactly what you wanted is not to negotiate; you are being manipulated by your ego or goals.

God's call to come back is a grace that eliminates your slavery to going away. God offers the guidance of the Holy Spirit to you who come back. Even more, God sets a table with the eucharist of Jesus, a foretaste of the fullness of the kingdom. Every coming back is a little taste of the eternal life that awaits you who hear God's call, "Come back!" and respond.

Meditation What was your most recent experience of going away and coming back? How was your going away a slavery? How was your coming back a freedom?

Prayer Holy One of Israel, when your people sinned, with great tenderness you called them back to yourself. With enduring love you pitied them. Many times I have gone away from your presence and sinned, but now I hear your call to come back. Open wide your arms to receive me. Guide my steps in the pathways of Jesus, the Redeemer.

Journal List the names of three people who have called you back. From what or where did each call you? List the names of three people whom you have called back. From what or where did you call each?

Promises

S c r i p t u r e "All you who are thirsty,
   come to the water!
You who have no money,
   come, receive grain and eat;
Come, without paying and without cost,
   drink wine and milk!...
Come to me heedfully,
   listen, that you may have life.
I will renew with you the everlasting covenant,
   the benefits assured to David....
For just as from the heavens
   the rain and snow come down
And do not return there
   till they have watered the earth,
   making it fertile and fruitful,
Giving seed to him who sows
   and bread to him who eats,
So shall my word be
   that goes forth from my mouth;
It shall not return to me void,
   but shall do my will,
   achieving the end for which I sent it"
(Isaiah 55:1, 3, 10-11).

R C I A "Because of the renunciation of sin and the profession of faith, which form the one rite, the elect will not be baptized merely passively but will receive this great sacrament with the active resolve to renounce error and to hold fast to God. By their own personal act in the rite of renouncing sin and professing their faith, the elect, as was prefigured in the first covenant with the patriarchs, renounce sin and Satan in order to commit themselves for

79

ever to the promise of the Savior and to the mystery of the Trinity. By professing their faith before the celebrant and the entire community, the elect express the intention, developed to maturity during the preceding periods of initiation, to enter into a new covenant with Christ. Thus these adults embrace the faith that through divine help the Church has handed down, and are baptized in that faith" (par. 211).

Reflection When you promise, you declare you will either do something or refrain from doing something. "I promise I will never pull the cat's tail again," the three-year-old says to his mother. The teenagers say to each other, "I promise to go steady with you." A couple making their wedding vows promises love and faithfulness.

Once in history, God made a promise to David that his descendants would rule forever. Some of David's heirs were good rulers and some were not, but God nevertheless kept the promise. Even when the monarchy was destroyed, people never gave up hope that sooner or later a descendant of David would restore the people and their land to a glorious state like that of the time of David.

The promise to David was kept in the person of Jesus. Many people did not recognize him because they were hoping for a warrior-like king. They wanted a political Messiah who would restore the kingdom of David. God, however, was more interested in inaugurating God's own kingdom. Thus, Jesus preached the kingdom of God. Jesus was not interested in power, but in weakness. Jesus was not interested in wealth, but in poverty. The Son of God did not wage war in order to defeat his enemies; he willingly went to his death on a cross while preaching the peace of his Father's kingdom.

Baptism immerses you into God's kingdom as revealed by Jesus. The errors of power, wealth and war must be renounced, as you promise to hold fast to God. All deeds of evil are replaced with a commitment to the mystery of the Trinity. "I believe in the Father, the Son and the Holy Spirit," you declare. All else is of no significance in the face of such a promise.

As in the past, God promises to satisfy your every thirst with God's Word. In your life, God promises to make his word effective; it will grow and blossom and do God's will in your life. God's promise of a kingdom, which was made to David, is kept every time another person is baptized into the kingdom of God.

Meditation To whom did you most recently make a promise? What was the promise? How did you keep it? In which ways is your promise-keeping like God's?

Prayer God of promises, with David you entered into an everlasting covenant. You promised him his heirs would sit upon his throne and rule forever. In Jesus, your Son, you have kept this promise. He revealed your kingdom is not one of power and might, but made up of those who are baptized into weakness and lowliness. I have heard your word and I seek your kingdom. Renew in me the benefits assured to David and satisfy my thirst to do your will. Keep me faithful to the promises I make.

Journal Search through the Bible and find three promises that God made to people. Identify the promise and how God kept it. Also, identify what promises people made in return and how they kept their promises.

Wisdom

Scripture "Hear, O Israel, the commandments of life:
   listen, and know prudence!...
You have forsaken the fountain of wisdom!...
Learn where prudence is,
   where strength, where understanding;
That you may know also
   where are length of days, and life,
   where light of the eyes, and peace.
Who has found the place of wisdom,

who has entered into her treasuries?...
She is the book of the precepts of God,
    the law that endures forever;
All who cling to her will live,
    but those will die who forsake her"
(Baruch 3:9, 12, 14-15; 4:1).

RCIA "The rite of Christian initiation...is designed for adults who, after hearing the mystery of Christ proclaimed, consciously and freely seek the living God and enter the way of faith and conversion as the Holy Spirit opens their hearts. By God's help they will be strengthened spiritually during their preparation and at the proper time will receive the sacraments fruitfully" (par. 1).

Reflection Usually, you define a wise person as one who has accumulated knowledge in one or several fields. However, wisdom is also attributed to those who have an ability to discern the inner qualities of people or to analyze interpersonal human relationships. This type of wisdom is often referred to as insight. Common sense, the ability to make good decisions on a daily basis, can be called wisdom.

The prophet Baruch focuses on the many meanings of wisdom by asking about wisdom's source. All wisdom comes from God; it can be found in a concentrated form in the law God gave to the people of Israel. In other words, God's wisdom—the wisdom in which people can share—is found in God's word.

You can absorb God's wisdom by hearing God's word proclaimed in public gatherings and reading it in a private setting. The mystery of Christ, the wisdom of God, is revealed through the word. In God's great wisdom Jesus became human and showed us how to live according to God's word.

Jesus preached the wisdom of God's kingdom. He focused on God's work in the lives of people in the present moment. Teaching people how God was living in them, Jesus invited people to follow him through suffering and death. He revealed the wisdom of the cross through his obedience to his father's will. Faith, as Jesus illustrated it, is nothing less than trust in God's saving wisdom and power, which raised Jesus from the dead.

Today, many people claim to be wise, experts. We have time management experts, education experts, religious experts and so on. However, all expertise pales when confronted with God's wisdom as revealed in God's law and Jesus.

Meditation How do you define wisdom? What two examples from your life illustrate your definition?

Prayer God of wisdom, in order to teach your people the way of prudence, you gave them the commandments of life, the fountain of wisdom. Through your word you called people to faith and conversion. In the fullness of time, you sent your Son, Jesus, to be the enfleshment of wisdom. Help me to understand the words of his teaching. Convert my heart through his preaching. Strengthen me with the Holy Spirit as I prepare to celebrate his sacraments.

Journal List three people (living or dead) you consider to be truly wise. Characterize for each their wisdom. Be specific. What does each reveal about the wisdom of God?

Renewed

Scripture "...Thus says the Lord GOD: ...I will sprinkle clean water upon you to cleanse you from all your impurities, and from all your idols I will cleanse you. I will give you a new heart and place a new spirit within you, taking from your bodies your stony hearts and giving you natural hearts. I will put my spirit within you and make you live by my statutes, careful to observe my decrees. You shall live in the land I gave your fathers; you shall be my people, and I will be your God" (Ezekiel 36:22, 25-28).

RCIA "Either immersion or the pouring of water should be chosen for the rite [of baptism], whichever will serve in individual cases and in the various traditions and circumstances to ensure the clear understanding that this washing is not a mere purification rite but the sacrament of being joined to Christ" (par. 213).

Reflection When you are renewed, you are refreshed, changed and you see reality through a new pair of eyes. For most of us, vacation is a period of renewal, as we travel to a place where we have never been before, experience new things and come home with a new viewpoint. A course can renew you by causing you to see a particular topic differently. A friend pointing out your error can refresh and renew your spirit.

The prophet Ezekiel speaking for God, told the captive Israelites that God would release them as God had done when they were slaves in Egypt. Using images of newness and freshness, the prophet urged the people not to give up; their God would renew them.

The clean water sprinkled upon the people washes away the impurities of their sins. They are cleansed of the idols they had worshiped, as they returned to worship the one God. Their stony, rebellious hearts—that is, their refusal to follow the word of God—are turned to natural hearts; they begin to love the God whose name they had abandoned.

God breathes the Spirit into them. Whereas before they had been lifeless and dry, the Spirit breathes new life into them and makes them enthusiastic in serving God. They are re-created. Their captivity ends and they return to the land God had given to Abraham and Sarah, their ancestors.

The most important action of God, however, was the renaming of the Israelites as God's people. The covenant between the people and God is renewed; God again promises to be the God of Israel, and Israel again promises to be God's chosen people.

What the prophet spoke of comes to fulfillment in baptism. The Spirit-filled waters drown the sin and wash away the evil of your life. The preparation leading to baptism turns your disobedient, stony heart into a natural heart on fire with love for Jesus and his commandment to love God, neighbor and self.

Not only are you drowned in the Spirit-filled waters of baptism, you are raised to new life. The Holy Spirit re-creates you into the image of Jesus. You breathe of the Spirit, as you are directed by the Spirit. The postbaptismal anointing with chrism seals you with the sevenfold gift of the Spirit.

The journey to baptism leads you to a new land, where you follow Jesus. You sit at his eucharistic table and feast on his body and blood; you taste of the fullness of the promised land. The land flowing with milk and honey of the past cannot compare to the rich fare of God's kingdom.

You who were no one become someone—a member of the body of Christ through baptism. You enter the ranks of the chosen people of God, and God promises never to stop renewing you.

You, a newly baptized person, are called a "neophyte," which means "recently converted." Maybe it is more accurate to say that you have been recently renewed.

Meditation What has been your most recent experience of being renewed? How were you renewed or refreshed?

Prayer Lord God, when your people wandered away from you, you called them back through your prophets and renewed them in your love. Now, through the Church, you sprinkle the clean water of your grace upon me and cleanse me from all my sin. You replace my stony heart of disobedience with the natural heart of the obedience of your Son, Jesus. And you blow into me the Holy Spirit's breath of life. Keep me faithful to the baptismal promises I prepare to make. Strengthen me as one of your chosen people. And bring me to the promised land of your kingdom.

Journal What are the three most renewing experiences of your life? Identify for each the new insight or approach that caused a change to take place in your life.

Through Death to Life

Scripture "...[A]re you unaware that we who were baptized into Christ Jesus were baptized into his death? We were indeed buried with him through baptism into death, so that, just as Christ was raised from the dead by the glory of the Father, we too might live in newness of life.

"For if we have grown into union with him through a death like his, we shall also be united with him in the resurrection" (Romans 6:3-5).

RCIA "...[I]n the celebration of baptism the washing with water should take on its full importance as the sign of the mystical sharing in Christ's death and resurrection through which those who believe in his name die to sin and rise to eternal life" (par. 213).

Reflection The standard measurement for a grave is 34 inches wide, 90 inches long and 72 inches deep. These dimensions are similar to those of ancient baptismal fonts, which were sunken into the earth in a special room called a baptistry. Steps led down into the watery grave on one end and steps led up on the other end.

Baptismal candidates stripped off their clothes and descended into the water-filled grave. There they were immersed. They were baptized into the death of Christ; symbolically, they were buried with Christ. In other words, the baptismal font is like a tomb, into which a person is buried and declared dead to sin.

After the people descended into the watery grave and were immersed into the death-dealing waters, they were raised up. They walked out of the baptismal pool, using the steps on the other side. The new Christians came up alive dressed in white, so that just as Christ was raised from the dead, they might live a new life. Jesus was lifted up out of his tomb by the glory of God; the new Christians raised themselves up from the grave to begin to share in Christ's risen life.

Hence, the baptismal font is both a tomb and a womb. It

is a tomb insofar as you die in it. It is a womb insofar as it is the place where your new life begins. St. Augustine, the fifth-century bishop of ancient Hippo, Africa, called the baptismal font "the womb of the Church." From the baptismal font the children of the Church are given birth, he said.

Thus, in baptism you die and come to life with Christ. Death no longer has any power over you, since you have already died. However, this descending into the baptismal pool and rising begins a pattern traced throughout your life. Death and life in Christ is one descending and rising process. You die with Christ—once in baptism and hundreds of times thereafter. You rise with Christ—once in baptism and hundreds of times thereafter.

You descend into the process of change and conversion, and you rise to new life, seeing the world in new ways. You live your baptismal promises. Often times, you have to forgive and forget the old grudge you hold dear and rise to forgiveness. You have to turn loose the "good old days" and rise to face the new days ahead.

Even family and friends have to be released to death. When your parents die, when your friends move away to another city, when crises cause you despair, you die a little. But all this dying is a prelude to the new life that follows—new family in the form of in-laws, new friends, new ways of seeing reality.

When the inevitable day arrives, when you are placed in that 34-inch by 90-inch by 72-inch grave, it will be but the final death of a long series of deaths. However, on the other side of that death, there will be life—just as there has been life so many times before. Your final death and resurrection will be nothing other than the final trace of baptism in your life.

Meditation What was your most recent experience of death? What new life followed it? In other words, when did you most recently die and rise?

Prayer God of death and life, you did not spare your

only-begotten Son but permitted him to die on the cross and be buried in a tomb. However, three days later you raised him to new life. Through the waters of baptism you immerse me into his death and resurrection and give me a share in his eternal life. Keep me faithful to my baptismal promises as you continue to trace the pattern of the death and resurrection of Jesus in my life.

Journal What are the three major experiences of death and resurrection in your life? To what did you die? What new life did you find once you passed through death?

Earthquake
(Cycle A: 1993, 1996, 1999, etc.)

Scripture "After the sabbath, as the first day of the week was dawning, Mary Magdalene and the other Mary came to see the tomb. And behold, there was a great earthquake; for an angel of the Lord descended from heaven, approached, rolled back the stone, and sat upon it. His appearance was like lightning and his clothing was white as snow. Then the angel said to the women in reply, 'Do not be afraid! I know that you are seeking Jesus the crucified. He is not here, for he has been raised just as he said' " (Matthew 28:1-3, 5-6).

RCIA "The whole initiation must bear a markedly paschal character, since the initiation of Christians is the first sacramental sharing in Christ's dying and rising.... [T]he Easter Vigil should be regarded as the proper time for the sacraments of initiation" (par. 8).

Reflection A physical earthquake is a powerful force. Depending on its magnitude, an earthquake can either be a slight trembling or a force strong enough to destroy whole cities and create a tidal wave that can level coastal buildings.

The mention of an earthquake in the resurrection account is unique to Matthew's Gospel. In fact, the author of this Gospel mentions an earthquake taking place immediately after Jesus' death on the cross (cf. Matthew 27:51-54). The earthquake is a metaphor for the final age. As far as Matthew is concerned, the final age has arrived with the death and resurrection of Jesus of Nazareth.

However, there is another type of earthquake. Any experience which causes your worldview, perspective, way of perceiving things, way of thinking about reality to rock is an earthquake. It is an upheaval in your life; it changes you forever. It cannot be seen, but it is felt in the inner depths of who you really are.

Almost every earthquake experience seems to progress through four steps: (a) you fear change, you want to hang on to what is old and familiar; (b) you die to old ideas; you give up the old ways, resign, surrender, concede; (c) you embrace new life; a new horizon is seen; you realize the new is not so bad after all; you get excited about the new; (d) you tell others about your experience; the earthquake story is shared with others.

The new life of Jesus, which can't be seen, is as powerful as an earthquake. Through the long days of preparing for the sacraments of initiation, you are rocked by multiple realizations of who Jesus is and to what kind of life he calls you. Many different earthquakes have taken place. Each of these prepares for the most devastating one—baptism. In baptism you face death by being immersed into the waters. However, the watery tomb cracks open and becomes a womb that gives you birth to new and eternal life.

Meditation What was your most recent earthquake experience? What did you fear? To what did you have to die? What new life did you embrace? With whom did you share your earthquake story?

Prayer God of earthquakes, you have made the earth a home for all of your people. However, the act of creation is never finished, for the earth continues to take shape through your guiding hand. When your Son slept in death on the cross, a great earthquake announced his resurrection from the dead. Be with me through the earthquakes in my life. When your word calls me to conversion, help me respond. Guide me through death to new life. May the words I speak always tell the story of your great deeds in my life.

Journal In which ways is baptism like an earthquake? What fears do you have? To what must you die? What new life can you glimpse on the horizon? To whom will you first tell the story of your own baptism?

New Clothes
(Cycle B: 1994, 1997, 2000, etc.)

Scripture "When the sabbath was over, Mary Magdalene, Mary the mother of James, and Salome bought spices so that they might go and anoint [Jesus]. Very early when the sun had risen, on the first day of the week, they came to the tomb. They were saying to one another, 'Who will roll back the stone for us from the entrance to the tomb?' When they looked up, they saw that the stone had been rolled back; it was very large. On entering the tomb they saw a young man sitting on the right side, clothed in a white robe, and they were utterly amazed. He said to them, 'Do not be amazed! You seek Jesus of Nazareth, the crucified. He has been raised; he is not here' " (Mark 16:1-6).

RCIA "The baptismal washing is followed by rites that give expression to the effects of the sacrament just received. The anointing with chrism is a sign of the royal priesthood of the baptized and that they are now numbered in the company of the people of God. The clothing with the baptismal garment signifies the new dignity they have received. The presentation of a lighted candle shows that they are called to walk as befits the children of the light" (par. 214).

Reflection The young man sitting in Jesus' tomb is unique to Mark's Gospel, considered by most scholars to be the oldest of the good news narratives. Matthew changes the young man to an angel of the Lord (cf. Matthew 28:2) and Luke changes the young man to two men (cf. Luke 24:4). Two questions are raised by Mark's account of the Resurrection: Who is the young man? What is he doing in the tomb?

To answer these questions, you must search Mark's Gospel for internal clues. The clue to identifying the young man is found in the account of Jesus' betrayal and arrest. After Judas betrays Jesus and Jesus is arrested, all his disciples flee. Then, the author states, "Now a young man followed him wearing nothing but a linen cloth about his body. They seized him, but he left the cloth behind and ran off naked" (Mark 14:51-52).

In an attempt to identify the young man, remember that in Mark's Gospel Jesus dies all alone—without any of his disciples, followers or mother near his cross. The Markan Jesus believes even God has abandoned him, for he cries out, "My God, my God, why have you forsaken me?" (Mark 15:34). He has been abandoned by everyone except a centurion, who ironically declares what no one else has been able to figure out: "Truly this man was the Son of God!" (Mark 15:39).

Once Jesus dies on the cross, Pilate gives his body to Joseph of Arimathea. Then the author tells us, "Having bought a linen cloth, he took him down, wrapped him in the linen cloth and laid him in a tomb that had been hewn out of the rock. Then he rolled a stone against the entrance to the tomb" (Mark 15:46).

Furthermore, in order to identify the young man, remember that baptism in the first century was done by immersion in the nude. As described earlier, baptismal candidates stripped off their clothes before stepping into the baptismal font. Thus, the young man who runs away naked is a baptismal candidate. For the author of Mark's Gospel, the authentic follower of Jesus is the person who has experienced abandonment, like Jesus did. In fact, a disciple is one who may (and usually does) abandon Jesus, just as the disciples in Mark's Gospel did (cf. Mark 14:50). Baptism plunges a person into the mystery of abandonment, where, according to Mark, God can be found.

The young man reappears clothed in the white robe in which Jesus was wrapped. He has been baptized into the mystery of abandonment. He is in the tomb because he has died and risen with Christ. The way into the tomb is baptism through the experience of abandonment, just as Jesus experienced it. You die when you are abandoned, but new life is discovered once you walk through the experience.

The author of this Gospel is making a very subtle statement about resurrection. He is telling you that if you want to "see" resurrection, you should not go off looking for the body of Jesus, as the women did. You can "see" resurrection in the flesh and blood of those who have been baptized in the abandonment (the suffering and death) of Jesus. The crucified one is raised up every time another person is immersed into the watery tomb. As a sign of this resurrected life, you, the newly baptized, are clothed in dignity with a white garment. You sit on the edge of the tomb and declare, "He has been raised; he is not here" (Mark 16:6).

Meditation When did you most recently feel abandoned by God, by others? When did you most recently abandon God, another person?

Prayer God of abandonment, when your Son hung dying on the cross, he was abandoned by everyone. Yet, you did not forsake him, but you raised him up on the third day. When I feel like you have abandoned me, awaken me to the security of your presence. When I abandon you, accept my repentance with your unlimited forgiveness. Trace in my life the mystery of your presence in my experiences of abandonment, as you did in the life of Jesus, your Son.

Journal What are three major experiences of abandonment in your life? What did you learn from each experience about the mystery of abandonment?

Remember?
(Cycle C: 1995, 1998, 2001, etc.)

Scripture "...[A]t daybreak on the first day of the
week [the women who had come from Galilee with Jesus]
took the spices they had prepared and went to the tomb.
They found the stone rolled away from the tomb; but when
they entered, they did not find the body of the Lord Jesus.
While they were puzzling over this, behold, two men in
dazzling garments appeared to them. They were terrified
and bowed their faces to the ground. They said to them,
'Why do you seek the living one among the dead? He is not
here, but he has been raised. Remember what he said to you
while he was still in Galilee, that the Son of Man must be
handed over to sinners and be crucified, and rise on the third
day.' And they remembered his words" (Luke 24:1-8).

RCIA "In proximate preparation for the celebration of
the sacraments of initiation:
1. The elect are to be advised that on Holy Saturday they
should refrain from their usual activities, spend their time in
prayer and reflection, and, as far as they can, observe a fast"
(par. 185:1).

Reflection In today's fast-paced world, you list
things that need to be done so you won't forget to do them.
So, on your refrigerator you post your grocery list—items
you must remember to purchase at the grocery store. You
list chores—work around the home assigned to each
member of a family. On your desk lies a list of errands—
things to be done to keep life running smoothly, such as
paying the electric bill, having the oil changed in the car and
picking up the dry cleaning.

For you who are preparing for the sacraments of
initiation, Holy Saturday is set aside as a day to make a list.
Most specifically, it is a day set aside to pray and reflect on
what will take place in the evening during the Easter Vigil. It
is not a day to be making an Easter dinner menu and
shopping for the necessary ingredients. It is not a day to be

perusing shops for new clothes. Holy Saturday is not to be spent mowing the yard or cleaning the house.

This day, which comes but once a year, is to be set aside for praying, remembering and fasting. You pray best in quiet. Solitude offers God the opportunity to speak to your heart and open your eyes so that you can recognize what God wills.

Remembering involves the Scriptures. The women at the tomb, according to Luke's Gospel, are told to remember what Jesus said. It is important to remember what Jesus said and what happened to Jesus, because what happened to Jesus is what will be happening to you being initiated during the Easter Vigil. You will be plunged into his death and resurrection. You will be anointed with his Holy Spirit. You will be fed with his body and blood, the sacrament of his Easter presence.

Fasting cleanses the body so that you can focus. If you are never without food, then you can never know what hunger is all about. But there is a sweetness to the taste of food if you have done without it for a period of time. By imposing a fast on yourself, you begin to hunger for the word of God and for the body and blood of Jesus.

On Holy Saturday you can also fast from words. Useless chatter can be put aside. You should speak only what is absolutely necessary. After all, it is impossible to speak and listen attentively simultaneously!

A fast from worries is also appropriate for Holy Saturday. No one denies the practical side of preparing for the post-Easter Vigil celebration with family and friends or the next day's dinner or laundry that needs to be done, but this time delegate these responsibilities to others. Let someone else worry about all such things.

Meditation List the things that need to be done on Holy Saturday. To whom can you delegate each of these tasks?

Prayer God of the living, once your Son was put to death on the cross and laid in the tomb, the whole earth paused for a day of prayer, reflection and fasting. However, once the sabbath was over, the women discovered you had raised the Lord Jesus from the dead. Quiet my heart this day. Remove my anxieties. Draw me into prayer. Through my fasting, help me remember all you do for me.

Journal List what you need to pray about, reflect on and fast from in order to be prepared for the Easter Vigil.

Chapter Six

Period of Postbaptismal Catechesis or Mystagogy

"The final period extends through the whole Easter season and is devoted to the postbaptismal catechesis or mystagogy. It is a time for deepening the Christian experience for spiritual growth, and for entering more fully into the life and unity of the community" (*RCIA*, par. 7:4).

Baptism

Naming

Scripture "When Abram was ninety-nine years old, the LORD appeared to him and said: 'I am God the Almighty. Walk in my presence and be blameless. My covenant with you is this: you are to become the father of a host of nations. No longer shall you be called Abram; your name shall be Abraham, for I am making you the father of a host of nations. I will render you exceedingly fertile; I will make nations of you; kings shall stem from you. I will maintain my covenant with you and your descendants after you throughout the ages as an everlasting pact, to be your God and the God of your descendants after you'" (Genesis 17:1, 4-7).

RCIA "The rite of choosing a baptismal name may be celebrated on Holy Saturday.... The elect may choose a new name, which is either a traditional Christian name or a name of regional usage that is not incompatible with Christian beliefs. Where it seems better suited to the circumstances and the elect are not too numerous, the naming may consist simply in an explanation of the given name of each of the elect" (par. 200).

Reflection One of the most important things parents do after the birth of their child is naming their newborn baby. Naming is important because it identifies you as a unique individual (first name) belonging to a unique family (last name). Your name is written on your birth certificate; your name will be written on homework assignments, contracts, letters and so on until it is finally carved into your headstone. Throughout your life, you are identified by the name you received at birth.

Until the use of birth certificates, a newborn child did not officially receive a name until the baby was brought to the local church for baptism. While the parents may have already decided upon the child's name, the son or daughter did not receive it officially until the church's minister asked, "What name do you give to this child?" Once the parents responded with the name, that was the name the child had in the Christian community forever.

Abram received a new name as he entered into a covenant with God. Abram became Abraham. The addition of the "ham" to Abram's name changed the meaning. Abram means "the father is exalted," which serves as a description of Abram's lofty status as the father of the nation of Israel. Abraham means "the father of a multitude of nations," which describes the multiple descendants which issued from Abraham's line. Both names identify Abram (Abraham) among other Israelites. Both names describe him.

Besides naming people, we name pets, cities, parks, mountains and other things. This naming not only identifies but also describes a particular animal, city, park or mountain. The name carries a whole host of meanings and connotations and reasons why this is its name.

In some countries where people have names that are incompatible with Christian beliefs, the elect choose new names to indicate the conversion of their lives in preparation for baptism. Most likely, you will keep the name you were given at birth. But as you are immersed into the baptismal tomb, you will die to your old identity and rise with a new identity as a follower of Jesus.

Meditation Why did your parents give you your name? If you don't know, find out by asking your parents or another relative. In which ways does your name adequately describe you?

Prayer God of Abram, when you solemnly entered into covenant with your servant, you gave him a new name to describe what you would do for him. Later, you gave his wife, Sarai, the new name of Sarah to indicate her status as a princess of your chosen people. On the day of birth, through my parents naming me, you called me by name to serve you in faithfulness. Guide all my actions that they may reflect the name of Christian that I bear. Help me to live my identity as a follower of Christ, your Son.

Journal What does your first name mean? What does your last name mean? Find out by making a trip to your local library and locating books that give the etymology (history of the form) of names.

Choices

Scripture "Joshua gathered together all the tribes of Israel at Schechem, summoning their elders, their leaders, their judges and their officers. When they stood in ranks before God, Joshua addressed all the people: 'Thus says the LORD, the God of Israel: In times past your fathers, down to Terah, father of Abraham and Nahor, dwelt beyond the River and served other gods. If it does not please you to serve the LORD, decide today whom you will serve, the gods your fathers served beyond the River or the gods of the Amorites in whose country you are dwelling. As for me and my household, we will serve the LORD.'

"But the people answered, 'Far be it from us to forsake the LORD for the service of other gods....'

"Joshua in turn said to the people, 'You may not be able to serve the LORD, for he is a holy God; he is a jealous God....'

"But the people answered Joshua, 'We will still serve the LORD'" (Joshua 24:1-2, 15-16, 19, 21).

RCIA "The rite of [Christian] initiation is suited to a spiritual journey of adults that varies according to the many forms of God's grace, the free cooperation of the individuals, the action of the Church, and the circumstances of time and place" (par. 5).

Reflection Every day you choose. From the moment

you awaken and rise from bed, you make decisions. You choose what clothes to wear, food to eat, place to sit on the bus or train, where to park the car and so on. Most choices are simple options from which you must choose; most choices do not have many consequences.

Other choices do have consequences; these are considered to be much more serious. After a visit to your doctor about an illness, you must decide something that will affect the rest of your life. After dating each other for a time, a man and a woman must choose to continue dating, marry or go separate ways. The decision to place an elderly parent into a nursing home rather than keep the person in your or the parent's home is a choice with consequences.

One of the most serious choices you can make is to be initiated into the Church. You make it only after seriously reflecting upon your lifetime journey of faith. You examine the steps in the path you have taken; this path usually points in a definite direction and helps inform your choice about Christian initiation.

Every individual's pilgrimage of faith is different. It varies from person to person because God works through the experiences of everyone's life a little differently. One person's choice may reveal God's grace while another person's choice may not. God's presence takes many forms.

Your choice to be initiated into the Church through baptism must be made freely. It must not be for any other reason than that you will it in your heart. Outside family pressures, reasons of social convenience or going along with the group because everyone else is being baptized does not make a free choice.

Joshua, Moses' successor as leader of Israel, asked for a commitment from the people before they crossed the Jordan River into the promised land. The Israelites had to leave behind the security of the gods of their ancestors and promise to serve the one Lord God, in whose image no statue could be fashioned. Like their ancestors who had passed through the Sea of Reeds with the help of the Lord, the Israelites would pass through the Jordan River with the help of God.

Likewise, you who seek baptism must leave behind the past and walk through the waters of new life. This is not an easy choice to make. As Joshua reminded Israel, fidelity to God is not easy. God is a jealous God; God chooses people and loves them and possesses them, like a young man and a young woman jealously in love. To decide to serve the Lord is a choice that will affect the rest of your life; this choice has serious consequences.

You will be asked to adopt a life-style, a code of morality, a manner of behaving that is in keeping with the Church's position on such ethical issues as abortion, euthanasia, economic justice, war and peace, and human dignity. Serving the Lord as a Catholic implies that you will worship with your local community every Saturday evening or Sunday morning. You embark on a lifetime of receiving information about the Church, reading it and digesting it. You embark on a lifetime of being formed by the Church into the image of Jesus. Besides these obvious consequences, each of you will be able to name specific ones which will bear directly on the changes you must make in your life.

Meditation What are the consequences of your choice to be initiated into the Church?

Prayer God of Joshua, you filled your servant with your grace of leadership so that he might bring your chosen people across the Jordan River and into the promised land. Before they began to cross you asked them for a renewed pledge of their fidelity, and they promised to serve you forever. I believe you have chosen me to be initiated into the Church. Strengthen me in the choice I have made by pouring your grace into my life. Be with me as I leave behind the land of the past and walk through the waters of baptism to the new life of Jesus.

Journal List the three major choices of your life that brought you to the decision to be initiated into the Church. Identify how you think God was at work and how you freely cooperated in each.

Washing

Scripture "Naaman came with his horses and chariots and stopped at the door of Elisha's house. The prophet sent him the message: 'Go and wash seven times in the Jordan, and your flesh will heal, and you will be clean.' But Naaman went away angry, saying, 'I thought that he would surely come out and stand there to invoke the Lord his God, and would move his hand over the spot, and thus cure the leprosy....' With this, he turned about in anger and left.

"But his servants came up and reasoned with him. 'My father,' they said, 'if the prophet had told you to do something extraordinary, would you not have done it? All the more now, since he said to you, "Wash and be clean," should you do as he said.' So Naaman went down and plunged into the Jordan seven times at the word of the man of God. His flesh became again like the flesh of a little child, and he was clean.

"He returned with his whole retinue to the man of God. On his arrival he stood before him and said, 'Now I know that there is no God in all the earth, except in Israel' " (2 Kings 5:9-11, 13-15).

RCIA "The celebration of baptism has as its center and high point the baptismal washing and the invocation of the Holy Trinity. Beforehand there are rites that have an inherent relationship to the baptismal washing: first, the blessing of water, then the renunciation of sin by the elect, and their profession of faith. Following the baptismal washing, the effects received through this sacrament are given expression in the explanatory rites: the anointing with chrism (when confirmation does not immediately follow baptism), the clothing with a white garment, and the presentation of a lighted candle" (par. 209).

Reflection You probably do a lot of washing every day. In fact, you may do so much washing you easily lose track of how much water you use.

In the morning, you shower, which washes away sleep and baptizes you into the new day. Throughout the day you wash your hands repeatedly, especially before meals. In the evening, you may wash your face before sitting down for dinner.

Clothes, cars and carpets are washed. We wash windows, floors and doors. We wash pots, pans and dishes. You wash fruits and vegetables. Our waste is washed away. Water is used with abandon to make people and things clean.

Naaman was washed clean of his leprosy. Naaman was the army commander of the king of Aram, but he contacted leprosy—a type of contagious skin disease. Naaman was not an Israelite. His only hope for healing was the Israelite prophet, Elisha, who told him to simply plunge himself seven times into the Jordan River—a muddy and dirty stream.

At first Naaman refuses to obey the prophet. He would rather have had Elisha say some magic words and perform some magic ritual over the leprosy and cure him. However, healing is not Elisha's prerogative; this act belongs to God. With some coaxing from his servants, Naaman obeys the prophet.

He immerses himself into the Jordan River, the water course that once separated Israel from the promised land. Once the Israelites had crossed the river in triumph as its waters opened up for Joshua and the people to pass through. Elijah, Elisha's predecessor, had rolled up his cloak and touched the river and it opened up for him to pass. Likewise Naaman, with his leprosy, passes through the river and enters the promised land of faith.

This is one of the major points of the story: Naaman, a non-Israelite, believes in the one God of Israel, the only God in all the earth. Through his ritual washing, Naaman is cured of his leprosy *and* his lack of faith. The power of God works through the waters of the Jordan River.

Likewise, the power of God works through the waters of baptism. Before being immersed into the waters which wash you clean of sin, you make a profession of faith in the one God. Then you pass through the water into the promised land of faith. The crossing is not a magic act; it is the next step in the process of a lifetime of conversion and faith. Every time you wash yourself or anything, you are reminded of your washing in baptism. Through ordinary water God reveals divine power.

Meditation What is the most important washing ritual you engage in? In which ways can it function as a reminder of baptism?

Prayer God of Naaman, you revealed your healing power at the Jordan River as your servant heeded the command of Elisha, plunged into the waters seven times and professed his faith in you. During this day, awaken me to your presence in the water I use for cleansing. Make my shower a reminder of baptism. Enable me to recognize healing in the rivers and streams I will cross. Let the flow of water through my home be a reminder of your grace which floods my life.

Journal List the people and things washed in and around your home. Identify for each how the washing is like baptism or how it can function as a reminder of baptism.

Predestined

Scripture "We know that all things work for good for those who love God, who are called according to his purpose. For those he foreknew he also predestined to be conformed to the image of his Son, so that he might be the firstborn among many brothers [and sisters]. And those he predestined he also called; and those he called he also justified; and those he justified he also glorified" (Romans 8:28-30).

RCIA "...[T]he entire community must help the candidates and the catechumens throughout the process of initiation: during the period of the precatechumenate, the period of the catechumenate, the period of purification and enlightenment, and the period of postbaptismal catechesis or mystagogy" (par. 9).

Reflection Paul attributes a number of qualities to God in his letter to the Romans. The first of these is foreknowledge, the ability to know everything past, present and future. This is easy to understand, since there is no time with God. Time is a human limitation; with God all past, present and future simply are. Therefore, God foreknows everything.

God also predestines. Paul does not understand predestination in the classical Reformation definition, which states that some people have been predetermined for heaven and some for hell. Because of God's foreknowledge, God has predestined you to share the image of Jesus, the picture of who you were created to be.

Jesus is the renewed image of the Creator. This image was destroyed by the sin of the first people. Through God's own Son, the image has been restored. When you are baptized, you die in the water to your old image of sin and rise to the new image of Jesus.

God calls you to look like Jesus. All people are predestined, but no one is forced. God's call is issued in freedom. God respects your free will. You may respond by being baptized or you may choose to follow a different path.

God has justified you so that you can respond to God's call. Justification is nothing other than the reconciliation of the world by God. Some people think they have to earn forgiveness or they have to do something in order to be made ready for God. According to Paul, God has already justified you through Jesus' death and resurrection. You have already been set free from sin; you need only to respond to God's offer of grace, to hear God's call.

And there is still more to what God has done for you. Through the waters of baptism, you already share in the glory of Jesus' resurrection. Just as Jesus was delivered over to death but glorified by the Father, through baptism you are handed over to death and raised up by God to lead a new life.

Foreknowing, predestining, calling, justifying and glorifying are part of God's plan in which everything works together for the good of all people who are loved by God. Just as God makes everything work together, so the community of believers works together for the good of those who seek to respond to God. The entire Church is responsible for helping you seek the sacraments of initiation. This is done through presence—being with you; through prayer—praying with and for you; through example— showing you how to accept God's freely offered gifts; and through acceptance—warm, hospitable welcoming into the community of believers.

Meditation Identify three events in your life you believe function as signposts, markers which predestined (pointed) you toward the Church.

Prayer All-knowing God, with you there is no time, but you have chosen to reveal your plan of salvation throughout the ages. The image of your goodness, found in man and woman, was destroyed by sin, but you had already predestined all people to share in its renewed image through Jesus, your Son. Open my ears to hear your call. Help me to accept your gift of justification. Through the waters of baptism give me a share in the glory of the resurrection of Jesus.

Journal In which two ways have you heard God's call? In which two ways have you experienced God's justification (forgiveness)? In which two ways have you experienced the glory of the resurrection?

Living Stones

Scripture "Come to [the Lord], a living stone, rejected by human beings but chosen and precious in the sight of God, and, like living stones, let yourselves be built into a spiritual house to be a holy priesthood to offer spiritual sacrifices acceptable to God through Jesus Christ.

"...[Y]ou are 'a chosen race, a royal priesthood, a holy nation, a people of his own, so that you may announce the praises' of him who called you out of darkness into his wonderful light" (1 Peter 2:4-5, 9).

RCIA "Immediately after their profession of living faith in Christ's paschal mystery, the elect come forward and receive that mystery as expressed in the washing with water; thus once the elect have professed faith in the Father, Son, and Holy Spirit, invoked by the celebrant, the divine persons act so that those they have chosen receive divine adoption and become members of the people of God" (par. 212).

Reflection As you have probably observed, a brick or stone building under construction rises slowly from the earth. This type of structure cannot be built in a day or two because the mortar has to set on the first levels of brick or stone before the next levels can be placed upon them. Gradually, however, piece by piece the structure takes shape, and in time the building is finished.

Reflecting on this phenomenon, the author of the first letter of Peter used it as a metaphor to explain the Christian community. He saw Christ as the cornerstone of the building and every Christian as a brick or stone in the structure. Together, Christ and his people build a spiritual house, much like physical bricks and stones can form a visible church building.

In the spiritual house, all of God's people are referred to as chosen. Through Jesus, God has chosen all people to be God's people. Once God chose Israel; now God chooses everyone.

You are a member of the royal priesthood. This means

you are to serve and worship God through Christ. Jesus established the paschal mystery—the revelation of God's presence in his suffering, death and resurrection—and you find it being traced in your own life. By acknowledging the mystery of God's presence in suffering, death and resurrection, you function as priest, offering praise to God.

God makes you, a follower of the Son, into a holy nation. Holiness is not something that you can do on your own; it is what God does in your life as one of his people. This chosen status is celebrated in the Sacrament of Baptism, which plunges you into the paschal mystery. Through baptism you are called out of darkness into the light of God's own Son.

Just as parents adopt a child and claim that child as their own by naming it, meeting its needs, nurturing it, so does God adopt you through baptism. All adopted sons and daughters are like living stones, which form a house, a church. Through your faith in Jesus, you are placed piece by piece on Christ, the cornerstone. And you are cemented to others with the Holy Spirit.

Meditation In which ways are you a living stone? Explain each.

Prayer God our rock, you made your Son the cornerstone of the Church through his suffering, death and resurrection. Through the waters of baptism you choose countless men and women to continue his royal priesthood, as you make them your own holy people through the workings of the Holy Spirit. Shape me into a living stone so I might worthily be built as a spiritual house and offer to you the acceptable sacrifice of my life.

Journal List the metaphors (other than living stones) you think can be used to describe the Church. Briefly explain each.

Wedding

Scripture "...I heard something like the sound of a great multitude or the sound of rushing water or mighty peals of thunder, as they said:
'Alleluia!
The Lord has established his reign,
[our] God, the almighty.
Let us rejoice and be glad
and give him glory.
For the wedding day of the Lamb has come,
his bride has made herself ready.
She was allowed to wear
a bright, clean linen garment.'
(The linen represents the righteous deeds of the holy ones.)"
(Revelation 19:6-8).

RCIA "The neophytes are, as the term 'mystagogy' suggests, introduced into a fuller and more effective understanding of mysteries through the Gospel message they have learned and above all through their experience of the sacraments they have received. For they have truly been renewed in mind, tasted more deeply the sweetness of God's word, received the fellowship of the Holy Spirit, and grown to know the goodness of the Lord. Out of this experience, which belongs to Christians and increases as it is lived, they derive a new perception of the faith, of the Church, and of the world" (par. 245).

Reflection A wedding is always a joyous occasion. Relatives and friends come from far and near to be with the groom and bride. The day before, as last-minute preparations are made, there is a rehearsal and maybe a meal which brings the immediate family of the groom and the bride together.

On the day of the wedding, there is usually some type of religious service during which the man and woman exchange vows as husband and wife. A reception follows during which guests can greet the newlyweds. In some cases, a dinner and a dance may also be a part of the festivities.

Everyone dresses in special clothes for a wedding. The bride wears a white gown, usually with a white veil and train. The groom is dressed in a tuxedo. Bridesmaids are clothed in special matching dresses; groomsmen wear matching tuxedos. Dresses of just the right color and style are chosen by the mother of the bride and the mother of the groom, while the fathers of each usually don tuxedos.

Throughout the Bible the wedding metaphor is used to refer to the union between God and us. Just as a man and a woman choose to spend the rest of their lives with each other, so does God choose to spend God's life with us. The intimacy associated with marital love is also found in the closeness of God to us, God's chosen people. God is often said to be jealously in love with us.

The author of the Book of Revelation uses the wedding metaphor to talk about the union of Jesus and the Church. The groom is Christ, the Lamb; the bride is the Church, the corporate body of believers who have remained faithful during times of trial and persecution.

By referring to Christ as the Lamb, the author echoes the Exodus reference to the blood of the lamb, which, when smeared upon the Hebrews' doorposts, saved those within the house. According to John's Gospel, like the passover lamb, no bones of Jesus were broken while he hung dying on the cross. However, from his pierced side there flows water and blood, baptism and Eucharist, the sacraments of birth in the Church. Thus, not only is the Lamb the groom and the Church his bride, but the groom also gives birth to the bride, whom he claims as his own.

The wedding metaphor is used in the Sacrament of Baptism when you, a newly baptized person, receive a white garment. You are told you have been clothed in Christ, and you are exhorted to bring your garment unstained to the judgment seat of Jesus so you may have everlasting life. As the Book of Revelation makes clear, the white garment represents the good deeds of those who are followers (brides) of the Lamb.

Through Jesus' suffering, death and resurrection, God's reign has begun. Indeed, Jesus preached God's reign. Through baptism, you are initiated into the reign; that is, through baptism you are made a bride who is wed to the groom, the Lamb, Christ.

Meditation How are you like a bride, who has made herself ready for her wedding (baptismal) day?

Prayer Almighty God, you have established your reign through Jesus' suffering, death and resurrection and you have called me to be joined to you in covenant love through him. Fill me with your Holy Spirit that I might always rejoice and be glad and give you glory for this gift. Dress me in your grace that I might be ready for my wedding day with the Lamb.

Journal Besides the metaphor of bride (Church) and groom (Lamb, Christ), what other comparisons can you use to describe the relationship between the Church and Christ? Briefly describe each.

Discipleship

Scripture "...Jesus said to his disciples, 'Whoever wishes to come after me must deny himself [or herself], take up his [or her] cross, and follow me. For whoever wishes to save his [or her] life will lose it, but whoever loses his [or her] life for my sake will find it' " (Matthew 16:24-25).

RCIA "In their renunciation of sin and profession of faith those to be baptized express their explicit faith in the paschal mystery that has already been recalled in the blessing of water and that will be connoted by the words of the sacrament soon to be spoken by the baptizing minister" (par. 211).

Reflection A disciple is a person who follows a master in order to be taught by that master. By listening to the master's words, observing the master's actions and walking in the master's steps, the disciple hopes to acquire the qualities and abilities of the master.

Today, we refer to this relationship of disciple and master as a period of internship. Young doctors spend time as interns in hospitals where they observe older doctors and learn their techniques. A trainee in most businesses is a disciple who is put under the care of a trainer, a person who knows the job from beginning to end. Part of the requirements for teacher certification in most states consists of a teacher training program. Would-be teachers are put under the care of a master teacher, who guides them in the best ways of functioning in the classroom.

Any type of discipleship involves discipline. Indeed, the root of "discipline" is *disciplina* which means teaching, learning. Hence, a disciple needs training that corrects, molds or perfects mental faculties or moral character. Instruction leads to mastery.

Disciples of Jesus, according to the author of Matthew's Gospel, deny themselves—willing to be betrayed by others, even if this means death. Betrayal is one of Matthew's favorite themes. The experience of betrayal is what leads to Jesus' death; he is betrayed by Peter and Judas. As an authentic disciple of Jesus you accept betrayal, as Jesus did, because you acknowledge you are not the center of your own existence; God is the center of your existence, as Jesus preached and lived. To deny yourself is to disown yourself and submit to the will of God.

This submission usually entails the cross. While the text probably meant literally taking up the physical cross to Matthew's original audience, today you must carry other types of crosses. In a "me first" society, your cross might be consciously putting others ahead of yourself. Denying a "consumer mentality" may bring the cross of giving with open hands instead of grabbing, taking and closing fists. Taking up the cross of humility will entail acknowledging the gifts of others instead of walking all over them.

Following Jesus as a disciple is not an easy task and one that should not be begun without careful discernment. It is a definite affirmation of acceptance of the paschal mystery—the tracing of Jesus' suffering, death and resurrection in your life. In other words, what happened to Jesus, the master, is what will happen to you who are his disciples.

Any disciple of Jesus who attempts to save his or her life through bargaining, lying or refusing to accept death will end up losing it. On the surface it may look like you have preserved life, but you have not. The example is the master, who lost his life and discovered that it was saved by God. Trusting the will of God is the source of your strength, which will enable you to begin to look like the master.

Meditation What was your most recent experience of denying yourself, taking up your cross and following Jesus? What life did you lose? What life did you find?

Prayer God of the cross, you revealed the mystery of life in the suffering, death and resurrection of your Son, Jesus. Even though he was betrayed by his disciples, he embraced his cross to do your will. You demonstrated your faithfulness by raising him from the dead. Make me an authentic disciple. Strengthen my faith in Jesus' paschal mystery that I might follow him through death to life. Through my self-denial and my crosses form me into the image of Jesus.

Journal List three occasions when you have been betrayed by others. What feelings do you associate with each of these experiences? How did you attempt to save your life but lose it anyway? What new life did you find after you had embraced the cross?

Powerless

Scripture "...[P]eople were bringing children to [Jesus] that he might touch them, but the disciples rebuked them. When Jesus saw this he became indignant and said to them, 'Let the children come to me; do not prevent them, for the kingdom of God belongs to such as these. Amen, I say to you, whoever does not accept the kingdom of God like a child will not enter it.' Then he embraced them and blessed them, placing his hands on them" (Mark 10:13-16).

RCIA "A sponsor accompanies any candidate seeking admission as a catechumen. Sponsors are persons who have known and assisted the candidates and stand as witnesses to the candidates' moral character, faith, and intention" (par. 10).

Reflection The words we use change through time in both denotation and connotation. Denotation is a word's direct meaning; connotation is a word's implied meaning. For example, "child" means a young person. Denotatively, the word describes a youngster. Connotatively, "child" implies innocence.

However, this meaning was not true in the world of the first century. In Jesus' world, "child" connoted powerlessness. A child had no rights, was totally dependent upon parents, to whom the child was totally obedient. When a girl reached her teenage years, she was given away in marriage by her father, who often received a dowry (payment) from her intended spouse. When a boy reached his teenage years, he was brought into the company of men, taught a trade and helped to find "a good wife."

Thus, when the Markan Jesus declares the kingdom of God belongs to children, he is saying that God's kingdom is for those who are powerless. Not only is this a favorite Markan theme throughout Mark's Gospel, but it is enfleshed in the person of the Markan Jesus, who dies powerlessly on the cross.

This created a great stir among those who followed Jesus. To be told that one must become powerless in order to enter the kingdom of God made no sense. The way to get anything in the ancient world, just like today, was through power and position. It was a man's world of power, the right plays, knowing the right people, having social position, owning things, possessing capital and so on. What a shock to hear Jesus declare that whoever wanted to enter the kingdom of God must accept it like a child, powerlessly!

Such a perspective turned the known world upside down. It called for the conversion of one's usual way of viewing reality and the embracing of a new way. Leaving behind the world of power and embracing the world of powerlessness, like a child, was not the way people thought about the kingdom of God, but it is the way the Markan Jesus preaches it.

Meditation Identify one way you have given up power and embraced powerlessness as a follower of Jesus. What have you learned from this experience?

Prayer God of children, your own child, Jesus, declared your kingdom belongs to the powerless. When I am tempted by worldly power, remind me of the necessity to be dependent upon you alone. When I seek prestige, teach me the vulnerability needed to accept the gospel. Strengthen me to accept your kingdom powerlessly, like a child.

Journal List ten ways people seek power in the world today. Identify for each of these the corresponding powerlessness that ought to characterize a follower of Jesus.

Born From Above

Scripture "...[T]here was a Pharisee named Nicodemus, a ruler of the Jews. He came to Jesus at night.... Jesus...said to him, 'Amen, amen, I say to you, no one can see the kingdom of God, without being born from above.' Nicodemus said to him, 'How can a person once grown old be born again? Surely he cannot reenter his mother's womb and be born again, can he?' Jesus answered, 'Amen, amen, I say to you, no one can enter the kingdom of God without being born of water and Spirit. What is born of flesh is flesh and what is born of spirit is spirit' " (John 3:1-6).

RCIA "...[T]he renunciation of sin and the profession of faith are an apt prelude to baptism, the sacrament of that faith by which the elect hold fast to God and receive new birth from him" (par. 211).

Reflection When a word or an expression has more than one interpretation, the word or expression is called a double entendre. For example, a person may say to you, "This is a cool day." The speaker understands "cool" to mean chilly. You, however, interpret "cool" to mean "good," "nice" or "alright." The two of you might exchange dialogue for a few minutes before you realize you are misinterpreting what the other is saying.

The unique story of Nicodemus and Jesus is founded on a double entendre. Jesus talks about being born from above, while Nicodemus hears being physically born again. There is a difference between being born from above and being born again. It is humorous as the reader of the story stands back and observes Nicodemus misundertand Jesus and, simultaneously, come to understand the difference between the two expressions.

According to the Johannine Jesus, the way to see the kingdom of God is through faith in the only Son of God. The person who believes is born of the Spirit through the waters of baptism. This person is not born again, as if he or she reentered the womb and emerged. Jesus' type of birth is begotten by God, not of the flesh.

From your mother's womb, you are born only one time. From the Spirit of God, you are born from above many times—both before and after baptism. Faith is gradually accepted; it grows and blossoms in the course of time.

John illustrates this by his portrayal of Nicodemus. In this first of three scenes Nicodemus comes to Jesus at night because he does not understand, nor does he believe. Nicodemus is clouded in darkness.

Later in the Gospel, Nicodemus is among a crowd discussing the origins of the Messiah from Galilee (cf. John 7:40-52). As the discussion progresses about whether or not the Messiah could come from Galilee, Nicodemus makes his next step toward faith by asking the crowd, "Does our law condemn a person before it first hears him and finds out what he is doing?" In other words, "Before judgment is rendered, shouldn't you get the whole story?"

The third scene in which Nicodemus appears is Jesus' burial. Only John narrates the fact that "Nicodemus, the one who had first come to him at night, also came bringing a mixture of myrrh and aloes weighing about one hundred pounds" (19:39). Finally, Nicodemus, assisting Joseph of Arimathea, emerges from the darkness to the light of faith. By assisting in Jesus' burial, he demonstrates his allegiance to Jesus. Nicodemus has come to faith.

Nicodemus is a model for you on your pilgrimage of faith. It is a lifetime journey during which you are always and gradually emerging from misunderstanding to understanding, from darkness to light, from a weak faith to a stronger faith.

Meditation When did you most recently experience going from misunderstanding to understanding or from darkness to light or from a weak faith to a stronger faith in your lifetime pilgrimage?

Prayer God of Nicodemus, you helped the one who came during the night to emerge into the light of day and profess belief in your only-begotten Son. As Nicodemus was born from above, you poured out your gift of the Holy Spirit upon him to strengthen him. Guide my feet in your pathways. When I stray, lead me out of the darkness of sin into the light of truth. Through water and the Spirit I have become your child.

Journal John's Gospel contains many other double entendres. Read through the Gospel and locate two other double entendres. Identify for each what Jesus means and what the other person hears or understands. How do these accounts assist your understanding of the passage?

Confirmation

Gifts

> **Scripture** "The spirit of the LORD shall rest upon him:
> a spirit of wisdom and of understanding,
> A spirit of counsel and of strength,
> a spirit of knowledge and of fear of the LORD,
> and his delight shall be the fear of the LORD"
> (Isaiah 11:2-3).

RCIA "Godparents are persons chosen by the candidates on the basis of example, good qualities, and friendship, delegated by the local Christian community, and approved by the priest. It is the responsibility of godparents to show the candidates how to practice the Gospel in personal and social life, to sustain the candidates in moments of hesitancy and anxiety, to bear witness, and to guide the candidates' progress in the baptismal life" (par. 11).

Reflection Most of us give and receive gifts on Christmas, birthdays and anniversaries. We offer an authentic gift to another person out of love, care and concern for the other person. The physical gift tangibly represents the intangible gift of ourselves. For most of us, gift-giving is a sacred and precious activity.

Your godparent is a gift. A godparent offers a good

example, displays the qualities of leading a Christian life and extends a hand of friendship to you as you prepare for the Sacraments of Baptism, Confirmation and Holy Eucharist. He or she willingly shares his or her practice of the gospel with you as you join your godparent on this lifetime pilgrimage.

You, however, are a gift to your godparent. You are seeking support and witness from another. The hesitancy you share with your godparent can lead your godparent to new insights and understanding of the faith. You bring the gift of new perspective to a godparent. Thus, while your godparent is guiding you, you in turn guide the one who journeys with you.

The gifts of a godparent to you and you to a godparent are like the gifts of the Holy Spirit, which God shares with everyone. Like any other unique gift, given freely out of a desire to share ourselves with another, God gives the gifts of the Holy Spirit to us. God shares God's self with us through seven special gifts: wisdom, understanding, counsel, knowledge, fortitude, piety and fear of the Lord.

Wisdom is God's gift of insight, enabling you to discern the inner qualities of yourself and others and the ability to reflect on human relationships. Understanding is the capacity to apprehend the relationship of particular, daily experiences in the general work of the Holy Spirit in your life.

The ability to seek advice from your godparent and those more experienced in the spiritual life is the gift of counsel, while the gift of strength gives you the capacity to resist the forces of evil which lead us away from the baptismal life.

The gift of the spirit of knowledge refers to the ability to know the will of God through experience or association with others. Through your cognitive faculties God unfolds God's will so that you might know it and do it.

The first reference to the spirit of the fear of the Lord in the prophet Isaiah concerns piety, faithfulness. This gift of the Holy Spirit enables you to remain devout and maintain fidelity to your baptismal promises.

The second reference to delighting in the fear of the Lord in Isaiah is not about being scared of God. It is the ability to recognize that you are a creature and that God is the creator. In the face of such recognition, it calls forth the virtue of true humility.

These traditional seven gifts of the Holy Spirit are not meant to limit God's gifts to you. Many other gifts are given according to each person's personality. In fact, each person is given unique gifts to build up the community of believers. The gift you are is an attestation of the Holy Spirit.

Meditation What is your unique gift given to you by the Holy Spirit? How do you use it to build up the community of believers?

Prayer God of gifts, you anointed your only Son with the power of the Spirit at his baptism in the Jordan River. Through the waters of baptism and the oil of confirmation you anoint me with the same sevenfold Spirit gift. Pour out on me your spirit of wisdom and understanding, your spirit of counsel and strength, your spirit of knowledge and faithfulness, and give me delight in my fear of the Lord.

Journal How are your godparents gifts to you? How are you a gift to your godparents? What do these gifts reveal to you about God?

Anointed

Scripture "The spirit of the Lord GOD is upon me,
   because the LORD has anointed me;
He has sent me to bring glad tidings to the lowly,
   to heal the brokenhearted,
To proclaim liberty to the captives
   and release to the prisoners,
To announce a year of favor from the LORD
   and a day of vindication by our God,
   to comfort all who mourn;..."
(Isaiah 61:1-2).

RCIA "In accord with the ancient practice followed in the Roman liturgy, adults are not to be baptized without receiving confirmation immediately afterward, unless some serious reason stands in the way. The conjunction of the two celebrations signifies the unity of the paschal mystery, the close link between the mission of the Son and the outpouring of the Holy Spirit, and the connection between the two sacraments through which the Son and the Holy Spirit come with the Father to those who are baptized" (par. 215).

Reflection Today, when you think of oil, you might think of the billions of barrels flowing from the Persian Gulf, the oil well in the middle of a cornfield in Kansas, Texas or Oklahoma, or the bottles and cans of oil lining the shelves of an automotive store. You might think of a little can of three-in-one oil, which can be used to keep home appliances running smoothly.

Besides being used to make gasoline, burned as fuel in a furnace or made into asphalt, oil is the basis for many personal health-care products. You smear on sunblock lotion, usually an oily substance. A cream applied to an itch has an oil base.

In the Hebrew Scriptures, a king of Israel was usually anointed with a horn of oil. A container of olive oil was poured over his head until it ran onto his shoulders and covered his beard. The sweet-smelling oil was a sign that God had chosen this man to be king of his people. Also, God shared God's spirit with the new king and gave him a mission. Thus, the king was called the anointed of the Lord.

Immediately after baptism, you are anointed on the head with chrism, a sweet-smelling mixture made from olive oil and balsam or some other perfume. The anointing represents the gift of the Holy Spirit. You are immersed into Jesus' death and resurrection through baptism, and you are anointed with Jesus' post-Easter gift of the Holy Spirit in confirmation. The mission of Jesus and the Spirit become your mission.

Like Jesus, you, a neophyte (newly initiated), are sent to bring the good news of the Christian way of life to others, especially those looked down upon. You live the freedom of a child of God and offer this liberty to others. God's favor is proclaimed as those who mourn are comforted.

Put simply, the Spirit of God sends you forth to be, live and share what God has done for you. The end of every celebration of the Eucharist reminds you of this. The priest or deacon dismisses you, saying, "Go in the peace of Christ" or "The Mass is ended, go in peace" or "Go in peace to love and serve the Lord." In all three choices, the important word is "Go." You are sent forth on the same mission.

Meditation What is your particular mission? Explain.

Prayer God of anointings, you chose your kings, priests and prophets by anointing them with oil and pouring out your Spirit upon them. You have chosen me through the waters of baptism and anointed me with the chrism of salvation. Now, send me forth to bring your good news to the lowly, heal the brokenhearted, proclaim liberty to the captives and announce your year of favor. Fill me with the gifts of your Holy Spirit.

Journal How can you bring glad tidings to the lowly, heal the brokenhearted, proclaim liberty to the captives, announce a year of favor from the Lord, comfort all who mourn? Make a list for each category.

Poured Out

Scripture "...I will pour out
    my spirit upon all [hu]mankind.
Your sons and daughters shall prophesy,
    your old men shall dream dreams,
    your young men shall see visions;
Even upon the servants and the handmaids,
    in those days, I will pour out my spirit"
(Joel 3:1-2).

RCIA "1. During the period of evangelization and precatechumenate, the faithful should remember that for the Church and its members the supreme purpose of the apostolate is that Christ's message is made known to the world by word and deed and that his grace is communicated. They should therefore show themselves ready to give the candidates evidence of the spirit of the Christian community and to welcome them into their homes, into personal conversation, and into community gatherings" (par. 9:1).

Reflection You engage in some type of "pouring out" ritual every day. In the morning you pour out milk, juice, water or coffee from some container. When something is poured out, it is taken from one container and placed in another one.

Speaking for God, the prophet Joel declares that God will pour out the divine spirit upon all people, sharing with you God's own self. The result of this pouring out is that young and old alike, free and slave alike share in God's Spirit.

The Spirit is poured out in the Sacrament of Baptism, as you are immersed in water and the Spirit. Then, the Spirit is poured out again in the Sacrament of Confirmation as you are anointed and sealed with God's special gift. The Spirit makes you an agent for God; you are entrusted with God's good news.

Those who have already been fully initiated into the Church have an obligation to continue the process of pouring out the Spirit. People, community, reveal the message of Jesus through word and deed to you who are seeking initiation. The Christian community possesses a unique spirit, which can be a revelation of God's grace to you.

Members of the community of believers pour out the Spirit through hospitality. By inviting you into their homes, they share in the apostolate of the Church. When others are welcomed and made to feel comfortable in a new setting, those sharing hospitality are functioning like Jesus, who welcomed both saints and sinners into his inner circle.

By drawing others into personal conversations the faithful share in Church's mission. Personal conversation does not have to be about issues facing the contemporary Church, although they might be topics. Sharing your daily struggle to live a Christian life, listening to people talk about their joys and sorrows and seeking the truth, as Jesus did, can be ways of communicating God's grace.

The community gathering for religious and social functions enables the members to confirm and enhance their identity. No person lives a totally solitary life; everyone is engaged in relationship to others. It is important that relationships be made visible. Thus, believers gather for religious services as well as social events. The Spirit is poured out as people pray together and eat, dance or play together. Jesus entered into all these activities to show that God is present everywhere people are found.

Meditation How has the Christian community poured out its Spirit on you?

Prayer God of Joel, through your chosen prophet you promised the gift of your Holy Spirit. Through the paschal mystery of your Son, Jesus, you poured out the Holy Spirit upon all people. This day I witness sons and daughters prophesying, old men and women dreaming dreams, and young men and women seeing visions of what the future can be. Pour out your Spirit on me, that by my words and deeds I might make known the message of your Son, Jesus Christ.

Journal List the ways you have had the Holy Spirit poured out on you by being welcomed into the homes of other believers, into personal conversation and into community gatherings.

Hands

Scripture "Now when the apostles in Jerusalem heard that Samaria had accepted the word of God, they sent them Peter and John, who went down and prayed for them, that they might receive the holy Spirit, for it had not yet fallen upon any of them; they had only been baptized in the name of the Lord Jesus. Then they laid hands on them and they received the holy Spirit" (Acts 8:14-17).

RCIA "The rite that is called the rite of acceptance into the order of catechumens is of the utmost importance.... God showers his grace on the candidates, since the celebration manifests their desire publicly and marks their reception and first consecration by the Church" (par. 41).

Reflection You use your hands so often you probably take them for granted. Your hands are used to pull yourself out of bed in the morning. Your hands grasp the bar of soap you wash with. You use your hands to dry your body. You use your hands to comb your hair and brush your teeth.

You use your hands to eat. Your hands hold the spoon that scoops up the cereal in your bowl. You grasp a glass of milk or a cup of coffee in one hand while you hold the paper with the other. Your hand holds the pen while the other holds the paper.

You may refer to your work as manual labor. "Manual" comes from the Latin word *manus* meaning "hand." At work your hands may be used for typing, constructing, building, holding, placing.

Your hands are used for loving another. When greeting another person, you may shake the other's hand. A couple in love are seen together holding hands. An encouraging pat on the back is given with a hand.

Likewise, your hands can be used for violence. You slap another in a moment of anger. You can pull the trigger of a gun, wield a knife and take drugs with your hands.

Doctors use their hands to heal. A relative uses his or her

hands to comfort one in grief. Nurses use their hands to encourage and strengthen. Parents use their hands to cuddle their children. Hands hold books, newspapers and magazines for reading.

In every sacrament of the Church, either the bishop, priest or deacon lays on hands. This laying on of hands represents the calling forth of the Holy Spirit, who pours out God's grace upon God's people. During the catechumenate, the minister lays his hands on your head after blessing you. In silence, hands are laid on the head of a child before baptism. Likewise, the minister's hands are extended over the baptismal water as he invokes God's blessing and calls upon the Holy Spirit to fill the water of the font.

In the Sacrament of Confirmation, hands are extended over all the candidates while the community prays for the gifts of the Holy Spirit. The minister lays his hand on your head as he seals you with the gift of the Holy Spirit by anointing your head with chrism. Your godparent places his or her right hand on your right shoulder to indicate that he or she is also sharing the gift of the Spirit with you.

While reciting the Eucharistic Prayer, the bishop or priest extends his hands over the bread and wine and asks God to send the Holy Spirit to change the elements into the body and blood of Christ. One of the forms of blessing at the end of Mass calls for the minister to extend his hands over the congregation as he asks God to bless the people.

In matrimony, the witnessing minister extends his hands over the couple for the nuptial blessing. When ordaining a man to the diaconate, the bishop lays his hands on the head of the candidate. When ordaining a priest, the bishop is joined by other priests in laying hands on the candidate. And a newly ordained bishop has had the hands of many other bishops placed on his head during the ordination ceremony.

When celebrating the Sacrament of Penance, the minister extends his hand over your head or lays it directly upon your head. Before anointing the sick, the minister lays his hands on the head of the ill person.

Meditation What is the most important way that you use your hands? Why? Explain.

Prayer Almighty God, when you created man and woman you gave them hands with which to touch, heal and comfort. When Peter and John visited Samaria, they called upon the gift of your Spirit by laying their hands upon the people. Lay your hands upon me and fill me with the gift of the Holy Spirit. Inspire me to do what is good, and make me strong, loving, wise and faithful in your service.

Journal How have you used your hands today? List the ways. How did you experience sharing the Holy Spirit through your hands?

Justified

Scripture "...[S]ince we have been justified by faith, we have peace with God through our Lord Jesus Christ, through whom we have gained access [by faith] to this grace in which we stand, and we boast in hope of the glory of God.... [A]nd hope does not disappoint, because the love of God has been poured out into our hearts through the holy Spirit that has been given to us" (Romans 5:1-2, 5).

RCIA "Although the rite of initiation begins with admission to the catechumenate, the preceding period or precatechumenate is of great importance.... It is a time of evangelization: faithfully and constantly the living God is proclaimed and Jesus Christ whom he has sent for the salvation of all. Thus those who are not yet Christians, their hearts opened by the Holy Spirit, may believe and be freely converted to the Lord and commit themselves sincerely to him. For he who is the way, the truth, and the life fulfills all their spiritual expectations, indeed infinitely surpasses them" (par. 36).

Reflection Justification is the act, process or state of being made right or acceptable to God by God. Justification is not something you can do on your own, nor is it a state of acceptability you can earn by obedience. God has already accomplished justification for the whole human race through Jesus. Reconciliation is God's gift of forgiveness or pardon to us. All you have to do is accept this gift.

Faith is your acceptance of this gift; you believe God has made you right in God's sight. Faith is not static, but it continues to reveal to you the next step of your lifelong process of conversion. Justification will reach its completion on the day of resurrection, a non-disappointing hope that God has poured into your heart through the Holy Spirit.

In the individualized world of today, however, you may fall into the trap of self-justification; you may believe you must earn salvation as if it has not already been offered to you. So, you seek to prove to God you are worthy of salvation by your good works or observance of the law. Good works and observance of the law are not bad in themselves; it is only when they are believed to be the vehicles of salvation that they lead you down the wrong path.

The commercial world thrives on selling salvation. Various beauty products are supposed to save you from wrinkles and age. Wheat, oat and corn bran are said to protect you from cancer. Low cholesterol products will save you from heart problems. Hundreds of types of pills, prescribed and sold over the counter, are hailed as miracle drugs. Living in such a world, you can see how you can be led to believe you can save yourself.

For you in the process of conversion, however, every day presents a new opportunity for you to recognize the deception of self-salvation. Jesus has saved all of us. God loves all of us and offers to us the gift of the Spirit; all that you have to do is respond to this gift with faith. Salvation is already given now; its fullness will be revealed in the resurrection.

Meditation In which three major ways do you find you attempt to save yourself? Identify how you can change each of these.

Prayer God of justification, you sent your Son, Jesus, that you might offer your gift of salvation to all people. Through his suffering, death and resurrection, you reconciled all people to yourself. You poured out your love in people through your Holy Spirit, who calls forth from them a response of faith. Continue to open my heart to deeper faith that I might be converted to you and sincerely commit myself to Jesus.

Journal List the reasons you think it is so difficult for people to accept God's gift of justification, respond with faith and live in certain, Christian hope.

Benefits

Scripture "There are different kinds of spiritual gifts but the same Spirit; there are different forms of service but the same Lord; there are different workings but the same God who produces all of them in everyone. To each individual the manifestation of the Spirit is given for some benefit.... [O]ne and the same Spirit produces all of these [gifts], distributing them individually to each person as he wishes.

"As a body is one though it has many parts, and all the parts of the body, though many, are one body, so also Christ. For in one Spirit we were all baptized into one body,...and we were all given to drink of one Spirit" (1 Corinthians 12:4-7, 11-13).

RCIA "The period of postbaptismal catechesis is of great significance for both the neophytes and the rest of the faithful. Through it the neophytes, with the help of the godparents, should experience a full and joyful welcome into the community and enter into closer ties with the other faithful. The faithful, in turn, should derive from it a renewal of inspiration and of outlook" (par. 246).

Reflection When you say "benefits," you are most likely referring to what good will personally come to you. A benefit is an aid; it promotes well-being. In the workplace benefits can mean health insurance plans, dental plans, retirement policies, unemployment compensation, working conditions, vacation time and so on. The members of an organization may sponsor a car wash, a bake sale or some other type of social event to benefit a cause or person in need.

In his first letter to the Corinthians, Paul turns this understanding of benefits around. For him, a benefit is not something you are to receive, but a gift you are to give away. The different charisms (spiritual gifts, forms of service, workings) come from outside of you; that is, every gift is a manifestation of God's grace, a revelation of the Holy Spirit. Whatever gift you may be given by the Spirit is given for the benefit of others and not solely for the good of yourself.

If you are a good teacher, able to impart wisdom to others, your gift is a manifestation of the Spirit for the benefit of others. If you display great faith, your trust is not for your own benefit, but the gift is a revelation of the Spirit for the good of others. You may be able to accomplish great things because you have been given the gift of insight by the Spirit; this gift is for the benefit of others.

Whatever way the Spirit has chosen to manifest the Spirit's presence in you—an action which is done freely on the Spirit's part—it is the one Holy Spirit who distributes the charisms as the Spirit wishes. In this regard, every person is gifted differently for others' benefit.

The special gift you have received as a manifestation of the Spirit is to be used for the building up of the body of Christ, which is one—though it has many parts. Just as the human body is composed of many parts yet one body working together in harmony, the body of Christ is one body with many members. The different gifts of the various members benefit the whole body and keep it working as one.

This happens because all special gifts have one common source—the one Spirit of God. You are baptized into the one body of Christ. You are given to drink of the one Holy Spirit. Any type of individual claim or attempt at possessing your special gift is an attempted denial of the basic premise that your charism is a manifestation of the Spirit for the benefit of other members of the body of Christ. In other words, you can never own the gift given to you by the Spirit; it has been given to you so that you can share it with the other members of Christ's body. Thus, the body is always being built up and enhanced by the Spirit. You, a newly-baptized member, bring your gifts to share with the community into which you have been baptized. The community in turn continues to share its gifts with you. Thus, both you and the community are changed, renewed and inspired and benefit each other.

Meditation What is the special manifestation (gift) of the Spirit given to you for others' benefit? In which three ways have you used this gift for others?

Prayer God of all good gifts, through your Holy Spirit you have given to your people different kinds of spiritual gifts, different forms of service and different works. Whatever the manifestation of the Spirit, it is given for the benefit of others. Guide me in my use of your precious blessings. Help me use them wisely, to be of service to my brothers and sisters and to transparently display your constant work in my life.

Journal List the names of three people from the Christian community. Identify for each one his or her special gift or manifestation of the Spirit, in your opinion. How has each of these persons used the gifts to build up the body of Christ? How have you benefited from each person's gift? What does each person's gift reveal to you about the Spirit?

Risks

Scripture "[The kingdom of heaven] will be as when a man who was going on a journey called in his servants and entrusted his possessions to them. To one he gave five talents; to another, two; to a third, one—to each according to his ability. Then he went away. Immediately the one who received five talents went and traded with them, and made another five. Likewise, the one who received two made another two. But the man who received one went off and dug a hole in the ground and buried his master's money. After a long time the master of those servants came back and settled accounts with them.... [T]he one who had received the one talent came forward and said, 'Master, I knew you were a demanding person, harvesting where you did not plant and gathering where you did not scatter; so out of fear I went off and buried your talent in the ground. Here it is back.' His master said to him in reply, 'You wicked, lazy servant! So you knew that I harvest where I did not plant and gather where I did not scatter? Should you not then have put my money in the bank so that I could have got it back with interest on my return? Now then! Take the talent from him and give it to the one with ten. For to everyone who has, more will be given and he will grow rich; but from the one who has not, even what he has will be taken away. And throw this useless servant into the darkness outside, where there will be wailing and grinding of teeth' " (Matthew 25:14-19, 22-30).

RCIA "...[T]he people of God, as represented by the local Church, should understand and show by their concern that the initiation of adults is the responsibility of all the baptized. Therefore the community must always be fully prepared in the pursuit of its apostolic vocation to give help to those who are searching for Christ. In the various circumstances of daily life, even as in the apostolate, all the followers of Christ have the obligation of spreading the faith according to their abilities" (par. 9).

Reflection When you take a risk, you face the possibility of a loss or personal injury. You may invest money by purchasing a particular stock; the risk is that the stock price may later fall or rise or the stock market itself may reach an all-time low or all-time high. You may take a chance by hurrying through an amber light; you may make it through the intersection or you may get hit by traffic beginning to inch its way across the junction.

There are big risks and small risks. Every day you take small risks. Leaving home is risking the possibility a burglar may break in and steal your possessions during the day. Just getting in your car is risking injury on the road. Doing something right or wrong at work is a risk of getting a raise or getting fired.

Opposed to risk is security. Security is the state of being free of risk, free of danger, free of loss, free of the possibility of personal injury. If you are secure, you are without fear or anxiety, without want or deprivation.

Daily, you experience security; in fact, you need it to survive the risks you face. Your home is your place of security; there you know where everything is located. At home you feel confident, protected and secure. In the home children look for security in their parents. Even the family pet continues to return home because the security of food and water is offered there.

Your job is security; it provides the need to work, which satisfies the need for money to participate in the economy. Having money fosters security insofar as you are able to provide food, clothing and shelter for yourself and others.

Many of us look at faith as security rather than risk. However, the Matthean parable of the talents (Matthew 25:14-30) makes it clear that the kingdom of heaven is for those who are willing to risk. Three servants were entrusted with one man's possessions, according to each one's abilities. Two servants risked multiplying or losing the man's possessions by trading or investing. One servant dug a hole and buried the money; this one opted for security.

When the master returned home and demanded an accounting, the two servants who took the risk were praised for taking the risk. The one who opted for security revealed that he presupposed the master was a hard man. Acting on his presuppositions, he failed to take a risk. Fear dominated his life. As a result, what little he had was taken away from him and he was thrown out into the darkness.

Faith is a risk. You either believe or you do not believe. If you believe even a tiny bit, you have faith. Faith is taking a chance on God's promises. Faith is trusting that God is truthful. Searching through your life for revelations of God's steadfastness, you find not proofs, but you discover how God was present in the moment of a risk. The result is that the talents entrusted to you are doubled.

The entire Christian community must always be willing to risk sharing its faith with others. The responsibility for initiating new members into the Church belongs to all the baptized. This means that everyone who is fully initiated should be willing to risk sharing his or her faith with you, who seek the communion that is the Church. According to each person's abilities, he or she risks sharing his or her faith and the faith of the community of believers.

This is no easy risk to take. It may result in rejection. It may result in the enhancement of your faith. The result might be a painful change that an individual realizes is necessary. Both positive and negative results may occur because of the risk. But without taking the risk, you will never know if it was worth taking. Security fosters conformity; risk fosters growth. One person in the parable conformed to security and lost all he had; two risked it all and grew into the kingdom. According to the Matthean Jesus, the kingdom of heaven is prepared for you who are willing to take risks.

Meditation What has been the greatest risk that you have had to take in faith? How did you grow? How were you changed?

Prayer God of risks, throughout history you have entrusted the message of your kingdom to those who believe. You have remained faithful to your prophets, who have proclaimed your word. You have stood by your kings, who led your people to freedom. You raised Jesus, your Son, from the dead, after he risked the scandal of the cross. Give me a firm faith. Teach me to risk sharing the gifts I have received with others. Fill me with enthusiasm for your kingdom.

Journal What are the three major risks you have taken in your life? Identify for each what you risked and gained from the risk. Identify for each what you might have lost if you had failed to take the risk.

Teacher

Scripture "[Jesus] stood up to read and was handed a scroll of the prophet Isaiah. He unrolled the scroll and found the passage where it was written:
'The Spirit of the Lord is upon me,
because he has anointed me
to bring glad tidings to the poor.
He has sent me to proclaim liberty to captives
and recovery of sight to the blind,
to let the oppressed go free,
and to proclaim a year acceptable to the Lord.'
"Rolling up the scroll, he handed it back to the attendant and sat down, and the eyes of all in the synagogue looked intently at him. He said to them, 'Today this scripture passage is fulfilled in your hearing' " (Luke 4:16-21).

RCIA "Catechists...have an important office for the progress of the catechumens and for the growth of the community.... When they are teaching, catechists should see that their instruction is filled with the spirit of the Gospel, adapted to the liturgical signs and the cycle of the Church's year, suited to the needs of the catechumens, and as far as possible enriched by local traditions" (par. 16).

Reflection The words "catechist," "catechesis," "catechize," "catechism" and "catechumen" all come from the same Greek verb *katechein* meaning "to teach." A "catechist" is the person who teaches or instructs others. "Catechesis" is the oral instruction the "catechist" gives to others. The act of the "catechist" giving "catechesis" is "catechizing;" it usually consists of oral systematic instructions through the use of questions, answers, explanations and corrections.

The "catechist" may use a "catechism," a book or manual containing a written summary of religious doctrine often in the form of questions and answers. The person who reads the catechism or listens to the catechist giving catechesis is called a "catechumen." The catechumen receives Christian training in doctrine and discipline before being initiated into the Church.

While Matthew particularly portrays Jesus as a teacher, the author of Luke's Gospel presents him giving his first sermon as a catechist, who reaches back into the past and proclaims the fulfillment of Scripture in the present. Luke understands Jesus to be the fulfillment of Isaiah's predicted anointed one, who would have a great concern for the poor, the captive, the blind, the oppressed, and who would proclaim the kingdom of God.

The Lukan Jesus declares he is the fulfillment of Israel's hopes and expectations. The kingdom of God is present now in the teaching of Jesus. It is not an event to be awaited any longer; it is present in the hearing (reading) of the gospel.

The task of the catechist is to awaken you and the whole community of believers to the fact that the kingdom of God is indeed present now. By being grounded in the spirit of the gospel, your catechist brings it to you and demonstrates how it is fulfilled in your hearing.

Such catechizing is a give-and-take event; the catechist shares insights with you, the catechumen and the community, and you and the community share your insights with the catechist. The signs and cycle of the Church's year along with local traditions serve as interpreters of the gospel. Through mutual sharing, all are enriched and inspired by the gospel.

Like Jesus, catechists, catechumens and the community proclaim the Scriptures are fulfilled in each other's hearing. Now, in the present moment, God is active in your life through the anointing with the Spirit. Once the message is realized, we, God's Spirit-filled people, are sent on a mission, like Jesus, to bring glad tidings to the poor, to proclaim liberty to captives and recovery of sight to the blind, to let the oppressed go free and to proclaim every year as acceptable to God.

Meditation Identify one way in which you functioned as a catechist in the past. Of what did your catechesis consist? Who was your catechumen? What was your catechism?

Prayer God, you anointed your Son with your Spirit and made him a teacher of your word that your people might realize the presence of your kingdom. To the poor he brought glad tidings. To captives he proclaimed liberty. He restored the sight of the blind and let the oppressed go free. He named every year acceptable to you. Breathe into me the Spirit of Jesus that I might teach your truth by word and deed. Give me the wisdom to proclaim fearlessly that you have already established your kingdom.

Journal Open your Bible to Luke's Gospel and choose a passage. After reading it thoughtfully, answer this question: How is this Scripture passage fulfilled in my reading (hearing)? Explain.

Thirsty?

Scripture "On the last and greatest day of the feast [of Tabernacles], Jesus stood up and exclaimed, 'Let anyone who thirsts come to me and drink. Whoever believes in me, as scripture says:

"Rivers of living water will flow from within...."'

"He said this in reference to the Spirit that those who came to believe in him were to receive. There was, of course, no Spirit yet, because Jesus had not yet been glorified" (John 7:37-39).

RCIA "From evangelization, completed with the help of God, come the faith and initial conversion that cause a person to feel called away from sin and drawn into the mystery of God's love. The whole period of the precatechumenate is set aside for this evangelization, so that the genuine will to follow Christ and seek baptism may mature" (par. 37).

Reflection After spending an hour or more mowing the lawn on a hot day, you are thirsty; you want something to drink. After playing tennis, baseball, softball, football, or swimming, you want the dry sensation in your mouth quenched with some cool liquid. After hiking a trail or going for an evening walk, you become thirsty. In most cases, you drink water to quench your thirst.

Besides thirsting for water, however, you also thirst for life. You yearn to be more than who you currently are. You want to give birth to new ideas, travel to new places, get to know new people. This thirst for more life reveals your thirst for God. Through daily activities and relationships, you sense there must be more than what is seen on the surface; this more is God.

After their escape from Egypt and while they were wandering in the desert, the Israelites began to thirst. Through Moses, God provided water from the rock for them. The thirst of the people was for more; they had left behind the security of slavery—there they had known who they were, they had food, they had water. In the insecurity of the desert, they were thirsty—they wanted to know who they were now; they needed food now; they wanted water now. All these were in relationship to the God who had led them forth from Egypt.

In time God offered Jesus to those who thirst for God.

Along the lifetime pilgrimage of faith, we get thirsty; we want more of God. Jesus came to satisfy this thirst. Whoever believes in Jesus and drinks deeply from the well of faith in him begins to flow like a river. The living water that Jesus gives is the Spirit, who is equated with water in John's Gospel.

When Jesus and Nicodemus meet for the first time in the dark of night, Jesus tells him that he must be born of water and the Spirit. Nicodemus must come to faith.

At Jacob's well, Jesus offers to give the Samaritan woman living water, a faith that will spring up within her. Finally, after she understands it is not he who is thirsty but she, she leaves her water jar and goes back into the town to tell others of the water that thoroughly quenches her thirst.

After Jesus dies on the cross, a soldier pierces his side and there flows out blood and water. For John, this is the climax of his Gospel. Through Jesus' death, resurrection, ascension and gift of the Spirit—one simultaneous event for John—the Church is born. Out of Christ's side comes the new Spirit-filled people of God. The Spirit leads and guides you on your journey of faith.

Meditation What has been your most recent thirst? How was it quenched? How do you think the Holy Spirit was active in this thirst?

Prayer God of the thirsty, in the desert you provided water from the rock to quench the thirst of your people and reveal your love for them. Through Jesus, your Son, you offered new birth through water to Nicodemus and living water to the woman of Samaria. Through the working of the Spirit, I have come to believe in Jesus. As I drink deeply of the sacraments flowing from his side, make me overflow with the living water of your grace. May I always thirst for you, the Triune God—Father, Son and Holy Spirit—living and reigning as one, for ever and ever.

Journal What are the three greatest thirsts in your life? How was each quenched? From what did you drink?

How has each of these experiences made your faith stronger or guided you in your journey of faith?

Eucharist

Bread

Scripture "...[I]n the desert the whole Israelite community grumbled against Moses and Aaron. The Israelites said to them, 'Would that we had died at the LORD's hand in the land of Egypt, as we sat by our fleshpots and ate our fill of bread! But you had to lead us into this desert to make the whole community die of famine!'

"Then the LORD said to Moses, 'I will now rain down bread from heaven for you....'

"In the morning a dew lay all about the camp, and when the dew evaporated, there on the surface of the desert were fine flakes like hoarfrost on the ground.... Moses told them, 'This is the bread which the LORD has given you to eat'" (Exodus 16:2-4, 13-15).

RCIA "The instruction that the catechumens receive during this period should be of a kind that while presenting Catholic teaching in its entirety also enlightens faith, directs the heart toward God, fosters participation in the liturgy, inspires apostolic activity, and nurtures a life completely in accord with the spirit of Christ" (par. 78).

Reflection The staple of almost every people is bread: shaped square, round or oblong; baked, fried or cooked; made from corn, wheat, rice or oats. In a time of famine, when nothing else is available, people rely upon bread as their sole, life-sustaining food.

Besides referring to food, bread can apply to Christian instruction. The information and formation you receive as you prepare for initiation is bread to be eaten and digested. This bread of training is a gift from the community of believers; it is meant to be consumed in its entirety.

The bread of instruction consists of an overview of all Catholic teaching. The entire body of teaching is like a loaf that cannot be eaten at one time but must be sliced and consumed in smaller portions. It will take you a lifetime to eat the entire loaf of Catholic instruction. This is why initiation is a lifelong process.

The bread of instruction enlightens your faith. It functions in the same way as a few crumbs serve to curb the hunger of the famished. Faith can be described as your hunger for God. The crumbs of instruction satisfy this hunger for a short time. You will, however, hunger for more. Thus, faith is always in need of instruction for enlightenment.

Your heart is directed to God through the bread of instruction. Just as bread can be a sign of the totality of foods when you give thanks for your daily bread, so too can the thanksgiving for instruction be a sign of your heart being focused on God and God's ways.

The bread of instruction fosters participation in the liturgy of the Church. When the community of believers gathers for public worship, the members break bread together. It may not be physical bread, as used when celebrating Eucharist, but it might be the bread of the word of God, the bread of forgiveness or the bread of healing. Whatever form this bread takes, it gives you the strength to praise God for God's activity in the world.

The strength received from the bread of instruction that fosters participation in the liturgy also inspires apostolic activity. This means that after eating you are sent forth to share your bread with others. Every liturgical service ends with a rite of sending forth. You share in the mission of the Church—to bring the bread of instruction and witness to others.

Finally, the bread of instruction nurtures the Christian

life. It enables you to be Christlike. Jesus, the bread from heaven, is God's gift to the world. You who follow him become bread, and you find yourself being broken and shared, just like Jesus was broken and shared as food for all people.

Meditation What has been your greatest source of bread in your life? Explain.

Prayer God of bread, when your people hungered for food in the desert, you satisfied them with bread from heaven, and you gave them the word of your instruction. Jesus, the teacher, was your new gift of bread from heaven. Give me an intense hunger for his Word. Instruct me and form me through your Church. Make me ready and willing to be broken and shared with all my brothers and sisters.

Journal Through the instruction you have received in Catholic teaching, identify one way in which your faith has been enlightened, one way in which your heart has been directed to God, one way in which your participation in the liturgy has been fostered, and one way in which you have been inspired to engage in apostolic activity.

Blood

Scripture "When Moses came to the people and related all the words and ordinances of the Lord, they all answered with one voice, 'We will do everything that the Lord has told us.' Moses then wrote down all the words of the Lord and, rising early the next day, he erected at the foot of the mountain an altar and twelve pillars for the twelve tribes of Israel. Then, having sent certain young men of the Israelites to offer holocausts and sacrifice young bulls as peace offerings to the Lord, Moses took half of the blood and put it in large bowls; the other half he splashed on the altar. Taking the book of the covenant, he read it aloud to the people, who answered, 'All that the LORD has said, we will heed and do.' Then he took the blood and sprinkled it on the people, saying, 'This is the blood of the covenant which the LORD has made with you in accordance with all these words of his' " (Exodus 24:3-8).

RCIA "As they become familiar with the Christian way of life and are helped by the example and support of sponsors, godparents, and the entire Christian community, the catechumens learn to turn more readily to God in prayer, to bear witness to the faith, in all things to keep their hopes set on Christ, to follow supernatural inspiration in their deeds, and to practice love of neighbor, even at the cost of self-renunciation" (par. 75:2).

Reflection If you cut your finger, blood begins to flow from the wound. When blood begins to flow, you see life pouring out of yourself. Blood is equated with life.

After a serious accident or during an operation, you may need a blood transfusion. The person who donates blood to another is said to give the gift of life. As the blood flows into the veins of another, you observe that life is pouring into the person. Blood is equated with life.

In the covenant-making ceremony of Exodus, the blood of animals is splashed on the altar, representing God, and on the Israelites. In this blood bath God and people are united as blood brothers and sisters. The blood of the animals represents the union of God and people. Their blood is intermingled; they are bonded together in a solemn covenant. The people agree to follow God's law, and God agrees to share God's life with the people.

As you are gradually initiated into the Church, you are taught how to share blood with the entire Christian community. The body of believers shares its blood with you through sponsors, godparents, prayer, witness and hope. As you receive this transfusion of Christ's life, you become bonded to the local parish, the diocese and the universal Church. As you practice love of neighbor, even to the point of self-renunciation, you begin the lifelong process of sharing blood with the other members of the Church.

Jesus demonstrated how the giving of blood is the sharing of life. According to the Gospel of John, after he died on the cross, Christ's side was pierced with a lance and blood and water flowed out. Through his life, Jesus shared the blood of his life with those who believed in him. On the cross, he gave his last drop of blood to indicate the new bonding between God and us.

The Holy Eucharist is the act of sharing in this new bonding through the blood of Jesus with the sacramental sign of red wine. The cup of wine is placed on the altar-table. The culmination of the sacraments of initiation is the coming forth of the newly baptized to share from the cup of the new covenant. In so doing, you say you will do everything Jesus has instructed. God says God will share eternal life with you who believe in Jesus.

Meditation What one experience of new life (blood transfusion) has flowed into your veins from the community of believers? What one experience of new life have you given to the community of believers?

Prayer God of blood, through the blood of holocausts and bulls you bound yourself in a life-giving covenant with your people, as they promised to obey your every word. Through the blood of the cross of Jesus, you made a new covenant with people and promised them the gift of eternal life. Make me always ready to share the blood of life with all people, even if it means self-renunciation. Keep me faithful to my baptismal covenant with you. Remind me that my flow of eternal life comes from you.

Journal List the three most important ways you think you have given life. What type of blood was involved in each? What transfusion did you receive from each?

Nourishment

Scripture "[Elijah]...went a day's journey into the desert, until he came to a broom tree and sat beneath it. He prayed for death: 'This is enough, O LORD! Take my life, for I am no better than my fathers.' He lay down and fell asleep under the broom tree, but then an angel touched him and ordered him to get up and eat. He looked and there at his head was a hearth cake and jug of water. After he ate and drank, he lay down again, but the angel of the LORD came back a second time, touched him, and ordered, 'Get up and eat, else the journey will be too long for you!' He got up, ate and drank; then strengthened by that food, he walked forty days and forty nights to the mountain of God, Horeb" (1 Kings 19:4-8).

RCIA "From this time on the Church embraces the catechumens as its own with a mother's love and concern. Joined to the Church, the catechumens are now part of the household of Christ, since the Church nourishes them with the word of God and sustains them by means of liturgical celebrations. The catechumens should be eager, then, to take part in celebrations of the word of God and to receive blessings and other sacramentals" (par. 47).

Reflection From the moment you were born, you sought nourishment. As a newborn infant you suckled at your mother's breast, sharing your mother's food and nourishing yourself. Then you ate soft, solid food—pabulum—which fostered growth. Later in your life, you consumed a balanced diet of proteins, carbohydrates and fats, used by the body to sustain growth and vital processes.

Like the sustenance needed for the body, you must also have nourishment for the mind. From your early childhood, your mind is fed with ideas and concepts. Your toys of plastic blocks of all shapes and sizes meant to be placed in corresponding indentations on a board were bread for your mind. Your parents read stories to you in order to nurture your imagination.

As an adult you read books, watch television, see movies, attend symphonies, peruse art exhibits and attend the theater to nourish your mind.

Just as your body and mind require physical food and food for thought to live, so does your spirit need spiritual food throughout your journey of faith. The first bite of spiritual food is the word of God. Through the inspired Scriptures God speaks to you. Indeed, this is spiritual pabulum the first time it is heard. Later in your life, when the word of God is studied and it makes its way to your heart, it becomes the solid foodstuff of the call to conversion.

Your spirit is also nourished through liturgical celebrations. The liturgy of the Church is the official, ritual, formal and public worship of the community of believers. It is official insofar as it is approved by ecclesial officials. It is ritual insofar as there is some repetition, which fosters a comfortable stance before God. The formal quality of liturgy removes it from the mundane and elevates it to a place of specialness. The members of the community engage in liturgy in public; it is visible to all. Thus, the meaning of the word "liturgy"—the work of the people—becomes clear. Through the work of worship, your spirit is replenished.

Your spirit can be nourished through blessings and sacramentals. When people or things are blessed, they are set aside as holy, to be used for sacred functions. They remind us of the holiness of God. Sacramentals, signs such as ashes, water and palm branches, function as reminders to you of who you have been called to be. These things are spiritual food.

Elijah needed spiritual food. After defeating the prophets of Baal and fleeing from the Mount Carmel area in order to preserve his life, he was spiritually depleted. He aad called upon the God of Israel to consume his offering, and God had taken not only the offering but the altar with it in one great fireball. But even with such signs, Elijah was tired and ready for death.

God fed Elijah under the broom tree in the desert, just as God provided manna for the Israelites in the desert after they had escaped from Egypt. With such simple gifts as a hearth cake and jug of water, the prophet was strengthened to walk to Horeb, the mountain of God's presence. The food in the desert was not just physical food for the body nor was it just another miracle to be pondered by the mind; it was spiritual nourishment for Elijah. God's tiny whispering voice on the mountain gave him the strength to return to his people and choose a successor, Elisha, who would continue to provide spiritual food for God's people.

Meditation When were you most recently nourished spiritually? Of what did this food consist? How did it strengthen you?

Prayer God of nourishment, when your people hungered for food, you not only satisfied their bodies, you gave them your covenant for their minds and your word for their hearts. When Elijah, your prophet, sat under the broom tree in the desert, spiritually depleted, you gave him the food that sustained him in your presence. Feed my spirit with your word; open up the treasures of the Scriptures for me. Through my union with others, help me to be spiritual nourishment for them.

Journal List the names of three people who have spiritually nourished you. How did each do this? What food did each offer to you? List the names of three people you think you have spiritually nourished. How did you do this? What food did you offer to each one?

Community

Scripture "[The community of believers]...devoted themselves to the teaching of the apostles and to the communal life, to the breaking of the bread and to the prayers.... All who believed were together and had all things in common; they would sell their property and possessions and divide them among all according to each one's need.

Every day they devoted themselves to meeting together in the temple area and to breaking bread in their homes" (Acts 2:42, 44-46).

R C I A "The third step of Christian initiation, the celebration of the sacraments, is followed by the final period, the period of postbaptismal catechesis or mystagogy. This is a time for the community and the neophytes together to grow in deepening their grasp of the paschal mystery and in making it part of their lives through meditation on the Gospel, sharing in the eucharist, and doing the works of charity. To strengthen the neophytes as they begin to walk in newness of life, the community of the faithful, their godparents, and their sponsors should give them... thoughtful and friendly help" (par. 244).

Reflection The family is the basic type of community. In its classical form it consists of a father, a mother and children. Today, this community may consist of a single-parent household or the union of two at-one-time-independent units.

Families form neighborhoods of homes, mow yards, talk across backyard fences and visit with each other in local parks. They have a sense of belonging and owning the neighborhood, and so they unite on various issues.

You may belong to service organizations, which are families devoted to particular projects on behalf of others. The leaders may refer to the group as "one big happy family."

When you are initiated into the Church through the Sacraments of Baptism, Confirmation and Holy Eucharist, you are brought into the community of believers. This parish family may be made up of small parish communities, which foster spiritual and educational growth among its members. A parish belongs to a larger community, identified as a diocese. Dioceses are grouped together in provinces and provinces form a country or nation. Nations are grouped together to form the universal Church.

Thus, initiation into the Church is simultaneously

immersion into the parish, the diocesan and the universal Church. You are not baptized simply to have a personal relationship with God—this is already presumed and understood. You are baptized into a community of believers who have duties to fulfill and obligations to meet for each other.

Together, the members of the Church on every level learn the teaching of the apostles. This consists of the lifetime religious education effort. It involves the study of the Scriptures, the history of the Church, an understanding of sacraments, perspectives on moral issues and so on.

A communal life requires the participation of the members of the Church in all types of activities, such as potluck dinners, dances, fund-raising for specific causes, committee work and so on.

A minimum of once a week the entire parish community gathers for the breaking of the bread, an early Church designation for celebrating the Sacrament of the Holy Eucharist. The Eucharist is where the community of the Church becomes visible, as all the many members who form the Church are made visible. Gathering for Eucharist in their diversity, the various members form one parish community and become a reflection of the diocesan communion of parishes and the world communion of the universal Church.

By devoting themselves to prayer, the members of the community strengthen their family ties. Some members may gather for morning or evening prayer in the local church building. Others may join together in prayer in special devotional services or meet in homes for time together. The cliche—"the family that prays together stays together"—is appropriate applied to the community of believers: The community of believers who prays together stays united as God's family.

Meditation In what situation have you most recently experienced community? Describe your experience. What was the experience of community like?

Prayer God of all believers, once you called a Hebrew

tribe to be your chosen community of faithful people. Through Jesus, you called all people to be united in one Spirit. Keep me faithful to the teaching of the apostles and the communal life, to the breaking of the bread and the prayers. Through my demonstration of unity may others come to believe in the name of your Son, the Lord Jesus Christ.

Journal How did you most powerfully experience the community of your parish; of your diocese; of the universal Church? Give one example of how you have experienced community through teaching, how you have experienced the communal life, how you have experienced community through the breaking of bread and how you have experienced community through prayer.

Lord's Supper

Scripture "...I received from the Lord what I also handed on to you, that the Lord Jesus, on the night he was handed over, took bread, and, after he had given thanks, broke it and said, 'This is my body that is for you. Do this in remembrance of me.' In the same way also the cup, after supper, saying, 'This cup is the new covenant in my blood. Do this, as often as you drink it, in remembrance of me.' For as often as you eat this bread and drink the cup, you proclaim the death of the Lord until he comes" (1 Corinthians 11:23-26).

RCIA "Just as their new participation in the sacraments enlightens the neophytes' understanding of the Scriptures, so too it increases their contact with the rest of the faithful and has an impact on the experience of the community. As a result, interaction between the neophytes and the faithful is made easier and more beneficial" (par. 246).

Reflection The Eucharist makes the community and

the community makes the Eucharist. The Eucharist makes the community insofar as we, the many different people who we are, gather together as a community to proclaim the death of the Lord as we wait for him to come again. We make the Eucharist insofar as we give thanks to God for the gift of Jesus, using the bread and the cup.

Paul's account of the institution of the Lord's Supper in his first Letter to the Corinthians is the earliest found in the New Testament. It is a statement that the death and resurrection of Jesus is for others. He gave his body and blood for others on the cross. He was raised to new life by God, who promised he would come again. So, in the Pauline Churches, the Eucharist made a community of believers who were waiting for the Lord to come. This waiting community celebrated the absence of Jesus, the one who had given his body and blood and promised to return.

The Markan account of the institution of the Lord's Supper places less emphasis on what Jesus did for the community and more on the Old Testament covenant-making ceremony. Mark relates, "While they were eating, he took bread, said the blessing, broke it, and gave it to them, and said, 'Take it; this is my body.' Then he took a cup, gave thanks, and gave it to them, and they all drank from it. He said to them, 'This is my blood of the covenant, which will be shed for many' " (Mark 14:22-25).

In Mark's account the disciples drink from the cup before Jesus interprets the action. For Mark, drinking from the cup implies participation in Jesus' suffering and death, which serves as a link between the covenant sealed in blood between the Israelites and God. Mark does not call this a new covenant; in his view, it is a continuation of the Exodus covenant sealed in blood.

Matthew, reworking Mark's account, relates, "While they were eating, Jesus took bread, said the blessing, broke it, and giving it to his disciples said, 'Take and eat; this is my body.' Then he took a cup, gave thanks, and gave it to them, saying, 'Drink from it, all of you, for this is my blood of the covenant, which will be shed on behalf of many for the forgiveness of sins' " (Matthew 26:26-28).

Matthew expands upon the meaning of the Lord's Supper by adding another interpretative angle. The disciples are told to take and eat the bread identified with Jesus' body. The command to drink from the cup is added by Matthew, while he omits the Markan disciples sharing the cup before Jesus interprets the meaning. Matthew adds the reason for the shedding of the blood of the covenant—the forgiveness of sins. Matthew understands the death of Jesus to be sacrificial: It takes place to free people from their sins.

Luke's account of the Lord's Supper presents two cups. Luke narrates, Jesus "took a cup, gave thanks, and said, 'Take this and share it among yourselves; for I tell you [that] from this time on I shall not drink of the fruit of the vine until the kingdom of God comes.' Then he took the bread, said the blessing, broke it, and gave it to them, saying, 'This is my body, which will be given for you; do this in memory of me.' And likewise the cup after they had eaten, saying, 'This cup is the new covenant in my blood, which will be shed for you' " (Luke 22:17-20).

Luke greatly expands the words interpreting the meaning of the breaking of the bread. Just as the body of Jesus was broken on the cross, so the broken bread serves as a reminder of what he did for people. Whenever we break the bread, we are to remember him. Also, only Luke interprets the covenant in blood as something "new." He, like Paul, understands that Jesus is inaugurating a new people of God. Just as Israel sealed the old covenant with blood in the desert, the new people of God seal the new covenant with the blood of Jesus.

In John's Gospel there is no institution account. The author of the fourth Gospel prefers to handle the institution of the Holy Eucharist with the sign of the feeding of the multitude and the interpretative discourse of Jesus following the narrative (cf. John 6:1-15, 22-71).

As the early Church took shape, the Eucharist that celebrated the memory of Jesus made the community; it formed the members of the community by emphasizing various aspects of the meaning of Jesus' death. Likewise, the community made the Eucharist; depending upon the understanding of the members, they invested Jesus' death with various meanings. This interpretative interaction continues today as you take your place around the Lord's table. You change the perspective as you are changed by the members of the Church. Thus the Church is always being enhanced by the addition of members to the body of Christ.

Meditation What does the following Memorial Acclamation mean to you: "When we eat this bread and drink this cup, we proclaim your death, Lord Jesus, until you come in glory"? To which account of the Lord's Supper does it more closely correspond?

Prayer God of the new covenant, you commanded that the paschal meal be celebrated so the community, born from the side of Christ on the cross, remembers the saving activity of your Son. By breaking bread I remember the broken body of Jesus. By drinking the cup of wine I renew the covenant sealed in his blood. Strengthen me with this food and drink, and form me into the image of Jesus, whose coming in glory I await.

Journal Get a copy of a missalette containing the Eucharistic Prayers used for Mass. Locate the institution narrative, the account of Jesus' giving his body as bread and his blood as wine to his disciples during his last Passover-Supper with them, in any one of the prayers. Compare it to those found in Paul's Letter to the Corinthians and in Mark's Gospel, Matthew's Gospel and Luke's Gospel. Note the similarities and the differences.

Mediator

Scripture "[Christ]...entered once for all into the sanctuary, not with the blood of goats and calves but with his own blood, thus obtaining eternal redemption. For if the blood of goats and bulls and the sprinkling of a heifer's ashes can sanctify those who are defiled so that their flesh is cleansed, how much more will the blood of Christ, who through the eternal spirit offered himself unblemished to God, cleanse our consciences from dead works to worship the living God.

"For this reason he is mediator of a new covenant: since a death has taken place for deliverance from transgressions under the first covenant, those who are called may receive the promised eternal inheritance" (Hebrews 9:12-15).

R C I A "In...eucharist the neophytes, now raised to the ranks of the royal priesthood, have an active part both in the general intercessions and, to the extent possible, in bringing the gifts to the altar. With the entire community they share in the offering of the sacrifice and say the Lord's Prayer, giving expression to the spirit of adoption as God's children that they have received in baptism" (par. 217).

R e f l e c t i o n A mediator is one who stands in the middle, functioning as an intermediary between two people or groups of people. The mediator attempts to bring about reconciliation through communication. A successful mediator effects a union between differing parties.

A parent may function as a mediator in a dispute between two children. There is one toy and two kids who want to play with it. By listening to the children and getting them to agree about the terms of the play, the parent functions as a mediator.

In the workplace professional men and women function as mediators between unions of workers and managers of companies. Sitting down at the bargaining table, the mediator listens to both groups and attempts a solution to benefit both sides.

Sometimes a mediator is called a counselor. A husband and wife find themselves involved in a dispute they cannot work out alone. So, they seek a counselor's advice, who listens to them, reflects back to them what they are saying and guides them to a solution.

The author of the Letter to the Hebrews understands

Jesus to be the mediator of a new covenant. He stood in the middle between God and people, and through his death he brought about reconciliation between both parties.

The covenant between God and people had been sealed in blood by Moses. Some of the blood had been poured on the altar (representing God) and the rest had been sprinkled upon the people to signify that God and people were united as blood brothers and sisters.

Jesus established a new covenant through the shedding of his blood. This new covenant was sealed in his blood on the cross. Even more, as heifer's ashes were used to cleanse a person of ritual impurity in the past (cf. Numbers 19:9, 14-21), how much more does the blood of Christ cleanse us of sin, which the old covenant could not effect. Now, through the blood of Christ, all transgressions are removed and we are heirs to God's promises.

You, who are fully initiated into the Church, share in the mediatorship of Christ every time you gather to celebrate the Eucharist. You remember how Jesus offered himself on the altar of the cross by doing the will of his Father. This act of selfless love demonstrated not only how much God loves you, but revealed how much you should love others.

The Letter to the Hebrews refers to Jesus as the new high priest who entered into the eternal temple of God's presence and offered the supreme sacrifice. However, he was not only priest, he was also the victim, the sacrifice. He offered himself for the forgiveness of sins and, in so doing, functioned as the mediator of the new covenant between God and us.

Every liturgical prayer expresses this unique mediatorship of Christ. Usually, the prayers of the Church are addressed to God the Father, but the request for whatever is needed is made through Jesus Christ. Most of them end this way: "We ask this through our Lord Jesus Christ, your Son, who lives and reigns with you and the Holy Spirit, one God, for ever and ever."

The Eucharistic Prayer gives thanks to the Father through his beloved Son, Jesus Christ. And every Eucharistic Prayer ends with some mention of how all good gifts come to people through Christ. The final words of every Eucharist Prayer are these: "Through him, with him, in him, in the unity of the Holy Spirit, all glory and honor is yours, almighty Father, for ever and ever." Whatever glory and honor is given to the Father is done so through the mediator, Jesus Christ.

Meditation What has been your most recent experience of functioning as a mediator? What did you do or say? What decision did you help others reach?

Prayer God of the new covenant, with the blood of bulls your servant, Moses, sealed the agreement between you and your people in the desert. With his own blood your only-begotten Son, Jesus, sealed the new covenant of your love on the cross. Through his death and resurrection you made him the new high priest and the eternal mediator between yourself and people. Cleanse my conscience of dead works and sins. Give me the grace I need to worship you in spirit and truth. Grant that I may receive the promised eternal inheritance of your kingdom.

Journal Identify three experiences of being involved in mediations. One should be of you functioning as mediator; two should be of a third party working with you and another or others. What was the issue in each experience? How did all the involved parties have to die a little? How did all the involved parties find new life?

Crumbs

Scripture "As the day was drawing to a close, the Twelve approached [Jesus] and said, 'Dismiss the crowd so that they can go to the surrounding villages and farms and find lodging and provisions; for we are in a deserted place here.' He said to them, 'Give them some food yourselves.' They replied, 'Five loaves and two fish are all we have, unless we ourselves go and buy food for all these people.' Now the men there numbered about five thousand. Then he said to his disciples, 'Have them sit down in groups of [about] fifty.' They did so and made them all sit down. Then taking the five loaves and the two fish, and looking up to heaven, he said the blessing over them, broke them, and gave them to the disciples to set before the crowd. They all ate and were satisfied. And when the leftover fragments were picked up, they filled twelve wicker baskets" (Luke 9:12-17).

RCIA "Since the Church's life is apostolic, catechumens should also learn how to work actively with others to spread the Gospel and build up the Church by the witness of their lives and by professing their faith" (par. 75:4).

Reflection You associate crumbs with small fragments of bread. When you open a loaf of cellophane-sealed white bread, a few crumbs fall out onto the counter. When you slice a freshly baked loaf of bread, crumbs are left on the breadboard. After eating, a few crumbs can be found on the floor around the table; these fell from the breadbasket as it was passed around. Usually, crumbs are whisked into the sink or swept up and thrown away.

Besides bread crumbs, there are also life crumbs. Life crumbs consist of the myriad experiences of your life, which, if remembered and reflected upon, can be solid food for your spiritual growth. This process consists of four steps: taking, blessing, breaking and giving.

First, you take a past experience of your life. Since life is filled with all types of personal encounters, thoughts, ideas and relationships, you need to choose but one for a given moment. By remembering the past experience, you take it and bring it into a new focus for the present time.

Second, you bless the experience—no matter whether it is labeled as a good experience or a bad one. To bless an experience is to thank God for enabling you to remember it. Furthermore, you thank God for permitting you to experience it. All experiences are gifts from God.

Third, you break open the experience. You spend some

time examining it, reflecting on its every curve and word. By opening it up and meditating on it, you crack it open for all it is worth. Things never seen before come into view. Words never heard before ring in your ears. That which was never touched is now felt.

Fourth, you give away the experience. You share it with others. It doesn't have to be shared by narrating the whole story. Many times you share a year's worth of your life by toasting another with a glass of wine. The totality of your experience is located in that simple glass of wine. Other times, you may share a meal with someone. A married couple can locate thirty years of life together in one meal. The fruit of your experience is shared with others.

When these four steps are taken, you discover you are immersed in some type of community, union with others. Like Jesus, who took the symbolic five loaves and two fish (making seven—a number signifying fullness) and gave them to the Twelve to be shared by five thousand, you take your experiences, bless them, break them and give them to the Church to be shared by all. Most of the time this is done through the celebration of the Holy Eucharist, using the signs of bread and wine.

Whenever the crumbs of your life are examined in this way, you discover signs of the presence of God. The sign might be the ocean, a sunset, a dinner, a glass of wine. It might be the sacred numbers seven or twelve. However, you can be assured that the taking, blessing, breaking and giving will reveal how God has been at work in your life.

It is always amazing how what looked like crumbs end up as loaves. The crumbs of your life yield baskets of leftovers. Not only will these serve as food for later, but they carry the potential to nourish others.

Meditation When did you most recently take a crumb of your life, bless it, break it and give it to others? What was the crumb? What sign did you use for the sharing of it with another or others?

Prayer God of crumbs, in a deserted place your Son,

Jesus, invited the apostles to feed the crowd with the crumbs of their lives. He showed them how to take, bless, break and give, and, thus, to recognize your presence in every daily experience. Give me the courage to take the past, thank you for it, break it open and share it with others. Form me into the image of Jesus, whom you have taken, blessed, broken and given for me.

Journal Identify the most important experience (crumb) of your life. First, record it in as much detail as you want. Second, write a prayer of thanksgiving to God for it. Third, break it open by reflecting on its meaning for you. Record all that it means. Fourth, through some sign share the fruit, joy or lesson of this experience with another or others. Fifth, identify your leftovers.

Recognition

Scripture "Now that very day two of them were going to a village seven miles from Jerusalem called Emmaus, and they were conversing about all the things that had occurred. And it happened that while they were conversing and debating, Jesus himself drew near and walked with them, but their eyes were prevented from recognizing him.... As they approached the village to which they were going, he gave the impression that he was going on farther. But they urged him, 'Stay with us, for it is nearly evening and the day is almost over.' So he went in to stay with them. And it happened that, while he was with them at table, he took bread, said the blessing, broke it, and gave it to them. With that their eyes were opened and they recognized him, but he vanished from their sight.... So they set out at once and returned to Jerusalem where they found gathered together the eleven and those with them.... [T]he two recounted what had taken place on the way and how he was made known to them in the breaking of the bread" (Luke 24:13-16, 28-31, 33, 35).

RCIA "When in communion they receive the body that was given for us and the blood that was shed, the neophytes are strengthened in the gifts they have already received and are given a foretaste of the eternal banquet" (par. 217).

Reflection Recognition is nothing other than the knowledge or feeling that someone present has been met before.

While shopping in a grocery store, you may wield your cart down an aisle and recognize someone leaning over the frozen food compartment. You and the other person recognize each other and identify each other by name. While mingling at a social gathering, you spend a lot of time recognizing others; you acknowledge another's presence and attempt to remember the other's name.

If you are waiting in an airport, bus station or train station, someone may come to you and say, "Hello! Remember me?" You immediately attempt to place the greeter in a city, office or neighborhood in order to identify and recognize this person. Obviously, the person offering the greeting has recognized you!

In Luke's unique post-Resurrection account of the travelers on the road to Emmaus there are two persons who do not recognize the risen Jesus among them. He is portrayed as a stranger, who happens to join them for the seven-mile walk. The point of Luke's story is not to explain why the two did not immediately recognize Jesus, but to portray how the early Christian community came to acknowledge his post-Resurrection presence.

When the travelers sit down at table with Jesus, he takes the bread, blesses it, breaks it and gives it to them. With these actions, they recognize him. What Luke is saying is if you want to recognize Jesus, you join the community for the breaking of the bread. The risen Jesus is acknowledged when the Church gathers together for Eucharist. And just as we recognize Jesus—that is, just as soon as our eyes are opened—he disappears from our sight. Thus, we will want to return to break bread again in the hope of recognizing him once more.

Today, the Church continues to break bread together in order to recognize the risen Lord. The whole Church is on a pilgrimage. You who seek initiation join the rest of the body of Christ as it makes its way through time. You who have known Jesus in the breaking of the bread teach those who are new to the journey how to do it. Continually, the whole Church foretastes the banquet of eternal life.

As you gradually recognize Jesus in the breaking of the bread, you begin to acknowledge him in other daily experiences.

In the face of the poor, you discover Jesus. Those who are sick and suffering from AIDS, cancer or any other disease become signs of his presence. The risen Lord is recognized wherever the members of his body—the Church—are found.

Meditation How have you most recently recognized the risen Jesus?

Prayer God of pilgrimages, when your people wandered in the desert, you fed them with manna from heaven that they might recognize you in your mighty works. In the person of Jesus of Nazareth, you have given us another sign of your presence. Open my eyes to see the face of Jesus in the poor, the suffering and the despised of the world. When I recognize him in the breaking of the bread, help me to acknowledge him in all of my brothers and sisters.

Journal When did you most recently join the community for the breaking of the bread? List the ways you recognized the risen Christ during the celebration.

True Food and True Drink

Scripture "Jesus said..., 'Amen, amen, I say to you, unless you eat the flesh of the Son of Man and drink his blood, you do not have life within you. Whoever eats my flesh and drinks my blood has eternal life, and I will raise him [or her] on the last day. For my flesh is true food, and my blood is true drink' " (John 6:53-55).

R C I A "...[I]n the celebration of the eucharist, as they take part for the first time and with full right, the newly baptized reach the culminating point in their Christian initiation" (par. 217).

R e f l e c t i o n John uses two double entendres in the bread of life discourse—flesh and blood. One group of hearers understands flesh and blood to refer to that which makes up a body; a human body is composed of flesh and blood. When the Johannine Jesus tells his listeners they must eat his flesh and drink his blood, they conclude he is talking about cannibalism.

Another group of hearers understands flesh and blood as a reference to bread and wine. Eating Jesus' flesh and drinking his blood is done with the sacramental signs of bread and wine. In this understanding, Jesus' flesh is true food (bread) and his blood is true drink (wine).

John's Gospel makes this latter interpretation clear when Jesus dies on the cross. He gives his flesh as food for the life of the world. He gives his blood, when his side is pierced and it flows forth, as sustaining drink for eternal life. Just as bread and wine are the staples of earthly life, Jesus' body and blood are the staples of eternal life.

The culminating point of Christian initiation is sharing this true food and drink. You gather around the table with Jesus and his friends and understand that eternal life is the result of eating the right bread and drinking the right wine—the body and blood of Jesus. You join the rest of the Christian community in eating the living bread and drinking the living wine, an act which enables you to live forever.

The Holy Spirit gives the true food and true drink of the Holy Eucharist just as with the gifts of Baptism and Confirmation. In every Eucharistic Prayer, the bishop or priest asks God to send the Holy Spirit to change the gifts of bread and wine into the body and blood of Christ. There is no magic here, only the ongoing activity of God in the world.

Just as the blessed water for baptism still looks and feels like water but is filled with the birth-giving power of the Spirit, and just as the consecrated chrism oil used in confirmation still looks and feels like olive oil but overflows with the sweet-smelling seal of the Spirit, so do the elements of bread and wine retain their physical characteristics. However, you who eat and drink are simultaneously expressing your unity and being united through the work of the Spirit. This type of Spirit-food enables you to live forever.

Meditation When did you most recently share food and drink with another person or other people? How did the conversation, food, drink and table unite you? What are the similarities between ordinary shared meals of food and drink and eucharistic shared meals of food and drink?

Prayer God, our true food and drink, you loved your people so much that in the desert you fed them with manna, bread from heaven. This food was a sign of your abundant grace, your desire to share yourself with your creation. Jesus, your Son, gave us his flesh to eat and his blood to drink as his greatest demonstration of love. As I approach your holy table to share his true food and true drink, fill me with the binding force of the Holy Spirit that I might be one with the community of faith.

Journal Search John's Gospel for three more double entendres. For each word or phrase identify the various meanings and how the different persons in the Gospel interpret the various meanings.

Chapter Seven

Pentecost

Lifetime Pilgrimage

Scripture "When the time for Pentecost was fulfilled, [the apostles] were all in one place together. And suddenly there came from the sky a noise like a strong driving wind, and it filled the entire house in which they were. Then there appeared to them tongues as of fire, which parted and came to rest on each one of them. And they were all filled with the holy Spirit and began to speak in different tongues, as the Spirit enabled them to proclaim" (Acts 2:1-4).

RCIA "The initiation of catechumens is a gradual process that takes place within the community of the faithful. By joining the catechumens in reflecting on the value of the paschal mystery and by renewing their own conversion, the faithful provide an example that will help the catechumens to obey the Holy Spirit more generously" (par. 4).

"To close the period of postbaptismal catechesis, some sort of celebration should be held at the end of the Easter season near Pentecost Sunday; festivities in keeping with local custom may accompany the occasion" (par. 249).

Reflection Your life is a journey, a trip through time, a walk across the planet named earth. As a Christian you refer to this journey as a pilgrimage of faith. Year-by-year as you travel you grow in deeper understanding and more fully practice what you have come to believe.

This lifetime pilgrimage of faith is the work of God through the power of the Holy Spirit. At times along the trail of life you may be filled with the wind of change. You feel the need to move, seek a different job, add another career or explore a new hobby. Likewise, your spiritual life is filled with the restless wind that moves you to try new types of prayer, seek a spiritual director or read the religious classics. This mighty wind is like that which swept over the waters before the birth of creation or that which filled the entire house in which the first community of the followers of Jesus were staying. The great rush of wind is a sign of the Spirit of God creating and recreating the world. It is a sign of the Spirit of God giving birth to the Church.

Sometimes the experience of the Spirit is like fire, which lights the way, warms and enflames you. In the midst of the darkness of despair, a candle's flickering flame can touch your heart with hope. A crackling fire's warmth can remove the cold chill of a day gone awry. While feeling defeated, fire can renew your sense of purpose and direction in life. This fire is the sign of the presence of God, just like it was for Moses, who discovered new purpose in the burning bush. The fire of the Holy Spirit rests upon you every day.

You may experience the Spirit in speech. In the act of consoling or comforting another, you never know what to say. However, on occasion the right words escape from your lips and the hurt is soothed. When confronted with death, the silence of your presence is often enough; presence says what no words can adequately capture. After struggling with the words of a speech, homily or lecture, the audience's level of understanding surprises you. All of these events are experiences of the Spirit, who prompts you to speak in different tongues, yet enables you to hear others in the midst of an often babbling world. Thus, every time the right words are spoken, the confusion of the Tower of Babel is undone by the Holy Spirit.

While Pentecost Sunday ends the *formal* process of Christian initiation, it sets in motion your lifetime pilgrimage of faith. Through the course of the liturgical year, you travel through the mysteries of life and death during the thirty-four weeks of Ordinary Time. In Advent you wait for the second coming of the Lord with joyful hope and ardent longing. During Christmas you remember how he once came and inaugurated the kingdom of God. Lent finds you either preparing for the sacraments of initiation or preparing to renew your own conversion of life. Easter is a celebration of the new life offered by God through Jesus' Resurrection. The birthday of the Church is Pentecost, the yearly remembrance of the fact that the journey goes on and this pilgrimage is the work of the windy, fiery, wordy Spirit.

Meditation Where do you go from here? What is your next step in your pilgrimage of faith? In what ways is the Spirit prompting you to take this next step?

Prayer God of wind, fire and tongues, you released your creative power across the face of the earth and established signs of your presence everywhere. Be always re-creating me with the mighty wind of the Spirit. Enflame my heart with the warmth of your love. Loosen my tongue to proclaim the great deeds you accomplish in my time. As I make my lifetime pilgrimage of faith, guide my steps to your kingdom, where you live and reign with the Lord Jesus Christ, your Son, and the Holy Spirit, one God, for ever and ever.

Journal As you review your lifetime pilgrimage of faith to this moment, identify one experience you have had of being blown in a new direction by the Spirit's wind, one experience of being set on fire with renewal by the Spirit and one experience of being prompted by the Spirit to say the right words.

Index of Scripture Readings

The numbers in brackets indicate where in the Lectionary for Mass you can find the particular Bible passage cited in this book.

Index of Quotations From the
Rite of Christian Initiation of Adults

This index gives the page numbers for particular paragraphs quoted in this book from the *Rite of Christian Initiation of Adults*.